Bye Bye Bad Karma

Rewriting History
to Change the Future

*"The distinction between the past, present and future is
only a stubbornly persistent illusion."*
Albert Einstein

Mary Blake

Copyright © 2019 by Mary Blake

All rights reserved under International Copyright Conventions.
No part of this book may be used or reproduced
in any manner whatsoever
without written permission from the publisher.

Printed in the United States of America

Kora Press ® is a federally registered trademark.

ISBN (13) 978-0-9979047-4-1

Published by Kora Press ®
www.KoraPress.com

*The painting of the Brooklyn Bridge (page 229) is reproduced with
the kind permission of the artist, Patrick O'Brien*

Dedicated to everyone who
has ever said,
"It must be my karma."

Thank You!

I owe so much to the students and clients who travelled to other lifetimes, worked with Spirit, released karma and freely share their good news with the world. I am infinitely grateful to the wise Spirit who taught us to rewrite history, erase karma and change our future.

This book could never have been written without the encouragement, advice and support of some really special people:

>Debra Engle
>Dr. Erica Goodstone
>Celeste Snyder
>Ilene Kristen
>David Harding
>Dianne Y. Johnson
>Shari Brandt
>David Clarke
>Joanna Infeld

…and I mustn't forget Alexander Murray, my first metaphysical mentor, who helped uncover and refine talents I didn't know I had.

Contents

Thank You   5

Just So You'll Know   13

Chapter One: Unlikely Game Changer   17
    Tea and Empathy   18
    Initial Endeavor   20
    Talent Galore!   22
    Intimations of Things to Come   24
    Spiritual Midwifery   27
    Disorientation Squared   31
    Ruminations and Ramifications   32

Chapter Two: Super Class?   37
    From Africa in Chains   38
    To Be Sold & Let   40
    The Consumption Connection   42
    Decompression   43
    Salutary Repercussions   44
    Inner Doubts and Deliberations   46

Chapter Three: First Solo Flight   47
    Contact!   47
    Puberty Ritual   49
    Jungle Legend   50
    Phenomenal Results   51
    Fresh Out of Excuses   51
    Reluctant Convert   54

Chapter Four: There and Back Again   55
    Backwards—and How!   55
    From Hovel to Palace   58
    Soul Therapy   59

Back to a New Future   62
What Have We Wrought?   63

Chapter Five: At the Feet Of The Master   65
Logic Please   65
Right Religion Wrong Destination   66
Risk and Ruination   68
Stuck!   69

Chapter Six: Of Camels, Wives, and Other Treasures   71
Simon   73
At the Grove   74
Conversion of a Skeptic   74
Afterthoughts   76

Chapter Seven: Dodging the Medicine Man   77
Lost   77
Blond God   79
Cosmic Reassessment   82
Spiritual Jet Lag   83
Dark Feelings   84

Chapter Eight: New Digs, New Focus   87
Life and Hardships and Stew   88
Culture Shock   89
Like it Was   90

Chapter Nine: Voyaging as Spectator Sport   93
The Reluctant Farmer   95
Escape From The Farm   96
Down on the Delta   98
Fire!   100
Shopping as Therapy   101
Centenarian Advice   103
A Disastrous Sea Voyage   104

At Thor's Command   104
Transmutation of a Viking Soul   106
Instant Debriefing   108
Triangular Vibrations   109

Chapter Ten: Never on Sunday   111
Dark Beauty   112
    Mob Frenzy   114
    Reporter at Large   115
    Post Mortem   116

Chapter Eleven: Three Crazy Guys   117
    Something Special   117
    All Gone Wrong   119
    Rattler!   120
    Ad Hoc Epiphany   120

Chapter Twelve: Two For the Money   123
    The Elusive Thread   123
    The Big One   124
    A Princess and Her Castle   126
    Queen Anne   127
    On the Happiness Trail   129
    For the Love of Annabelle   130
    The Silver Lining   132

Chapter Thirteen: High Stakes and Burning Questions   135
    Offhand Comment or Prophecy?   137
    Unexpected Apology   137
    Pros, Cons & Responsibility   139

Chapter Fourteen: Sifting the Sands of Time   141
    Vanishing Phobia   141
    Villain or Savior?   142
    New Challenges   144

Chapter Fifteen: Accidental Encounter   147
    A Gift From Heaven   147
    Celantine and the Betrayer   148
    Interview on a Dungeon Wall   149
    A Calculated Seduction   150
    A Brilliant Strategy   152
    A Peaceful Departure   154
    Pathways to Understanding   155
    Retracing, Refining and Evaluating   157

Chapter Sixteen: Sharpening My Saw   161
    Credentials at Last!   162
    A Transient Gleam   163

Chapter Seventeen: Al Fresco Healing   165
    Hanged Man   166
    A Young Tough   167
    A Different Game Plan   168
    Payback Time   171
    Change Upon Change   172
    Reality or Illusion   174

Chapter Eighteen: A Girl With Lives and Lives and Lives   177
    A Tenuous Commitment   178
    A Tentative First Voyage   180
    Bound to Service   182
    Tragedy!   183
    Summing Up   184
    More Questions Than Answers   185

Chapter Nineteen: Toonshi   187
    Them   188
    Chipping Away   190
    Monitoring Progress   191
    Evolving Concepts   192

Chapter Twenty: What If Everything Goes Wrong? 195
    Between the Furrows 195
    A Hint of Avarice 197
    How Profound 198
    Don't Knock It, It's Working! 199
    Results Trump Methodology 200

Chapter Twenty-One: A Professional Challenge 203
    A Difference of Opinion 203
    Silent Witness 204
    Professional Confirmation 205
    Counting the Ways 206
    Unresolved Questions 207

Chapter Twenty-Two: Into the Dark Side 111
    The Method 211
    The Village Market 212
    A Humble Abode 213
    A Dangerous Mistake 215
    Spirit to the Rescue 218
    Pledge of Honor 220
    Triumphant Entry 222
    Results… and More 224
    Spiritual Lessons Gratefully Acknowledged 225

Chapter Twenty-Three: A Bridge to Transformation 227
    The Limerick 228
    A Bridge to Transformation 228
    The War to End War 230
    Influenza! 232
    Time Between Time 234
    Theft or Liberation? 234
    Ethereal Pardon 236
    A Bitter Pill to Swallow 239
    The Sheikh Unmasked 241
    Revelations in Review 243

How I've Grown   245

Chapter Twenty-Four: Heal at Your Own Risk   247
Vishya   248
Mirror, Mirror   251
Rumors and Gossip   252
Survival Training   255
When In Rome   257
A Fresh Start   258
Closure   259

Chapter Twenty-Five: The Importance of Being Open   265
Reality in Flux   266
Consciousness Redefined   267

Just So You'll Know

I was born in the Bible Belt, where miracles stopped dead at the end of *Revelations* and Jesus was the only one who could heal, period. What was I supposed to do when an errant bolt of lightning shot down our living room wall and activated my latent healing ability? Like most of you who were drawn to this book, I spent way too much time trying to fit into society's version of normal and denying my true nature. In my little town people who didn't fit in or chafed against the status quo were either ridiculed or pitied. We were weird—the misfits, dreamers, malcontents, wishful thinkers or rebels.

Most of us waste way too much energy pretending everything's okay when it's really not. Our intuition and inner knowing tells us one thing and our parents, teachers and friends say the exact opposite. Our creativity, unique talent and gifts are crammed into a mold of conformity. When our true nature peeks through, we're told to stop daydreaming and memorize those multiplication tables and dates.

We're told exactly how life is and will always be: "Some are stuck with bad luck; it's God's Will, or fate; life is a struggle and then you die." We weird ones live with doubt, denial and rationalization. It's better than wondering if we're crazy, but not nearly as good as knowing we're okay. No one ever suggested that society hadn't caught up with us yet.

I learned the hard way that I was weird. Somehow I knew to keep secret things, like the strangers who popped up now and then out of nowhere, or the odd-looking creatures that attended my tea parties. At three, the fire that burned down our tent activated karmic survival guilt from the 12th century. Of course, back then reincarnation and karma were unheard of in southern Illinois.

Along the way, most of us experience odd events—impulses, attractions/aversions, déjà vu, chills, premonitions, warnings or hunches. The lucky ones eventually encounter kindred spirits. Sometimes a book or a course will strike a chord and inspire a hunger to seek knowledge beyond what traditional education and conventional wisdom have to offer. Often it takes a crisis, a disaster or a "wake-up call from God" to open our minds and hearts to the search for greater truths, deeper meaning, higher standards and goals.

At 15, I got my first wake-up call. A single lightning bolt out of a cloudless sky ripped down the living room wall three feet from me. My grandfather, who was in the kitchen, was paralyzed for several minutes. It lifted my brother's bed one and a half feet off the floor, tore one-third of the shingles off the roof, and filled the house with black smoke. I, being the closest, received the greatest impact.

The healings began three weeks later. At first it felt weirder than usual, but I convinced myself they were ordinary massages. That theory got me through half a lifetime. Eventually evidence became so overwhelming it coalesced into an unavoidable truth. In 1969 my yoga teacher told me one of my massages "fixed his back." He'd suffered excruciating pain from WWII shrapnel wounds for over twenty years. Nine years later a spontaneous cure of my own lung cancer by a fellow healer forced me to accept that God-given talent and dedicate my life to using it to help others.

Once the commitment was made, new doors opened; the pace accelerated. A universe of esoteric knowledge flooded my consciousness. I travelled to London in 1979 and attended 29 lectures by world famous experts at the Mind Body Spirit Festival. I was amazed at the outstanding talent "other people" had developed. One of the lecturers told me a massive shock often activated ESP abilities. The mystery of those first massages was solved. It took a bolt of lighting to set me on the path to my destiny—not so weird after all!

English healers accepted me and insisted they'd never encountered such powerful healing energy. It was hard to believe, since they had so much more experience than I. A psychic at the Spiritualist Association of Great Britain predicted I would develop a completely new technique for healing on a spiritual level and then would go on to do even greater work. I relegated her predictions to well-meaning flattery.

Back in New York, I found myself gravitating toward a spiritually-oriented community. In my determination to be a better instrument of Divine Purpose, I attended many classes, lectures and workshops. My

Bye Bye Bad Karma

new friends had a whole different vocabulary—tarot, astrology, karma. They introduced me to Alexander Murray, a gifted New York channel. I joined his classes and later interned with him. Those classes were a veritable crash course in metaphysical knowledge. I spent half a lifetime in denial, insisting I was an intellectual, a mother, a writer and a singer… not a healer. It took a series of spiritual breakthroughs to prepare me for the journey ahead. This, then, is how my Spirit-training began.

Chapter One
Unlikely Game Changer

Completely absorbed in transcribing taped channeling sessions, I barely noticed an unusually heavy snowfall. Murray, convinced no one in their right mind would brave such a storm, cancelled the class and insisted I spend the night on his couch.

The eerie silence was shattered by the doorbell. I opened the door and stared in disbelief at a half-frozen stranger. "I'm Lorna," she gasped," I'm not too late for class, am I?"

It seemed cruel to send her back out into the storm she'd braved to attend a cancelled class. I asked my mentor if it would be okay to offer her a cup of tea.

"Up to you, but I'm out of it," he sighed and, with a nod of consent, disappeared into his private quarters.

This photo from the Daily News shows intrepid firemen's struggle in midday. Just imagine what it would be after dark. That's how it was when karma snuck up on me.

Mary Blake

Tea and Empathy

Once the teakettle was on, Lorna leaned forward eagerly and asked if I was a psychic. When I assured her I was just a healer, not a psychic, she couldn't have been more pleased.

"A psychic told me I have healing ability," she confided.

Usually I'd have dismissed that as fortune teller flim-flam, but as her passion showed through, I reconsidered. She was a med student determined to integrate psychic healing into her future medical practice. "Professional validation is very important here in the States," I responded. "English healers often work side by side with medical doctors." She was amazed to learn that the UK medical system allowed them to work together for the good of the patient.

"Everywhere I went there were serious people involved in spiritual work. It was a relief to be accepted as normal. They introduced me as 'an American Healer.'"

Eager to learn everything at once, she peppered me with questions about my "psychic healing." I explained that I was a spiritual healer, not a psychic healer.

Her eyes widened. "Really! I didn't know there was a difference. It wasn't mentioned in anything I've read. How do you know you're a spiritual healer?"

I explained that I'd learned it accidentally in the most exciting workshop I'd ever attended. Itzhak (Ben) Bentov, author of *Stalking The Wild Pendulum*, had regaled us with tales about his scientific expedition to the Philippines. He had recruited world-famous scientists, surgeons, photographers and engineers to document the work of psychic surgeons.

"They were stunned into shock watching the healers at work," I giggled. "He said a world-famous surgeon sagged against a wall and blurted, 'Our whole goddamned system is no goddamned good!' After analyzing those phenomena, Bentov developed his revolutionary concept about healing: 'Spirit guides adapt their teachings to local customs so that people can believe they are healed.' Then he stated, 'Psychic healing stops at the neck. It's great for broken legs and other physical injuries, but it won't work on mental, emotional, or spiritually related conditions.' That felt wrong to me.

Bye Bye Bad Karma

"When someone asked if psychic healers could hurt a patient, Ben answered that the only way it could backfire was if the person being healed was strong and the healer was in a weakened condition. In that case the healer could possibly draw energy from the patient. At that point I couldn't contain myself. I stood to be recognized and respectfully submitted that if a psychic healer was tuned in to and channeling the Universal Healing Energy, great—sometimes dual—healings could occur, even if the healer were physically ill.

"'Aha!' Ben shouted, 'that's something else entirely! You just described a spiritual healer, not a psychic healer!' I bowed, thanked him for the promotion and almost fell back into my seat. Till then I didn't even know there was a difference!"

As we laughed about that surprising revelation, I glanced at the clock. "Lorna, look at the time," I exclaimed. "I'm afraid we've taken advantage of this gentleman's hospitality. We should call it a night."

"I know you're right," she sighed, "but I hate for this to end. I've learned so much, but I want more. Could I join your classes?"

It was flattering that this young med student considered me an expert, but I wasn't ready. After a lifetime of denial, the thought of teaching a healing class was daunting. As gracefully as possible, I sent her back out into the storm with a promise to be back next week for the channeling class.

As I tidied the kitchen, the energy lingered. Lorna's eager questions had stirred something usually kept locked away. It never occurred to me that she would be the catalyst to propel me into a future beyond my wildest dreams.

She attended Alex's next class and began a weeks-long crusade to persuade me to teach a healing class. None of my excuses—lack of location, experience or certification—deterred her. She offered to help organize the class and to do all she could to get it going. Finally it became easier to give in than to continue making excuses.

I wrestled with an avalanche of self-doubt. So far it would be a class of one with no curriculum, no classroom, and no track record.

Mary Blake

Initial Endeavor

Don, a grateful client, enthusiastically volunteered to make Lorna's project happen. In typical bulldozer fashion, he found a location for the class. I was suddenly out of excuses! As a spirit-trained healer, I'd never even attended a healing class. Now I had exactly one week to create a class agenda, a lesson plan, and find a volunteer for a healing demonstration.

We needed a "victim" for the class to practice on. It didn't seem appropriate to work with a client. A healing colleague was the logical choice. After several tentative phone calls, I got lucky. When Monique learned about the class, she said, "Sorry, can't come. I've got a broken ankle."

"Wonderful! " I whooped.

"What did you say?" she gasped.

Realizing how that sounded, I apologized and explained my dilemma. The opportunity to practice on a real injury was the answer to a prayer. "Are you game?" I asked.

"Why not," she sighed. "I'm in such physical discomfort I'd welcome any help I can get."

It was serendipity. Anything that happened that easily had to be right. My last excuse had just evaporated.

After a day of transcribing trance sessions for Alex, the deadline for Class Number One loomed imminent. I grabbed my pitiful notes and rushed headlong into the fray, wondering how it could possibly work.

How do you teach something totally instinctual? From that very first massage, every healing was spontaneous. My hands would automatically reach out and touch the right spot. I had no rules, formulae, or standard procedures. Years of random encounters were a very tenuous starting point. I'd just have to wing it and pray the class would work out as well as all those impromptu healings had.

I had only met Bernice, Don's friend whose apartment he'd preempted, once and didn't know what to expect. It was a fifth-floor walk-up studio dominated by a dramatic sheer-draped bed. She had set up a row of folding chairs in the center with an armchair and side table facing the class. There was just time to set up candles and incense to clear the air and fill the room with positive healing energy.

Bye Bye Bad Karma

Lorna arrived with a friend in tow. With barely contained excitement, she introduced Anna, who seemed a bit surprised at how normal I looked. Bobbi, a dancer I knew from Alex's classes, was next, followed by a woman I hadn't met. Much to my relief, we were a respectable class of five.

The class commenced to the rhythmic thud of cast and crutches on five flights of stairs. I began with basics: "Everyone is a healer unaware. All mothers kiss booboos. A hug makes you feel better when you're in pain, right?" I asked. Heads nodding on automatic bolstered my confidence.

"Let's affirm our intention to develop our unique gifts as instruments of healing. Close your eyes, relax, breathe deeply, float inside and focus on that thought," I instructed them. "We offer our services to be used for the greatest good," I solemnly intoned. The class repeated it word for word.

I "touched in" with each of them so they could experience channeled healing energy first-hand.

Monique finally arrived, exhausted by the climb, stashed her crutches and collapsed into the armchair. The agony of the swollen, throbbing ankle registered clearly on her lovely face.

Lorna stood, identified herself as a medical student and asked permission to examine her ankle to determine its condition before the healing began. "That way we'll be able to measure how well the healing works," she explained.

"Brilliant," I thought. That logical step hadn't occurred to me during my frantic preparations.

We couldn't have hoped for a better subject. Monique was accustomed to working with energy, which multiplies results. The energy already flowing through me intensified as I began to work. I described every step, explaining what I was doing and why. I instructed her to draw in the universal energy, direct it through her body and command the ankle to use that energy to heal itself. Monique, following my instructions with the confidence of a believer, absorbed the energy and set it to work.

Class members watched transfixed as the miraculous physical improvement began. The discoloration gradually faded; the swelling went down, and by the end of the healing, the stiffness had eased and she could move her ankle.

Lorna carefully re-examined the ankle and announced that from a medical standpoint, about ten days' healing had taken place in the course of 20 minutes.

Momentum built during the animated discussion that followed. The undeniable evidence that healing worked fueled their enthusiasm. Could they try it? Would it work for them? I encouraged them to experiment.

We were on a roll. The class was way beyond going well. The enthusiastic response, the excitement, the latent healing energy activated in one single class was just short of a miracle.

I asked each one to describe their personal reactions and impressions. They were surprised to discover the uniqueness of their individual experiences.

"I felt a rhythmic energy pulsing through me," Bobbi ventured.

"I was just standing there thinking nothing was going to happen," Anna confessed, "and then a strange feeling began moving down my arms. I've never felt anything like it before."

Others noticed a pulsing sensation, a warmth, a tingling or a relaxation. The clarity and depth of their awareness intensified by the minute. Experiential learning with observable results is as good as it gets.

I explained that everyone has different abilities and gifts. "Experiment; don't just copy what I do," I urged. "There is no one way to heal. It's a matter of what works… and don't be surprised if the response differs from one patient to another. Just don't forget to draw in the universal energy before you begin or you'll wind up exhausted."

I was determined to help them discover their unique healing talents and gain confidence in using them as quickly as possible. Learning by rote represses and distorts creativity. Here was a chance for them to discover and use their own gifts, rather than merely follow a regimented system step by step.

Talent Galore!

The excitement of revelation and self-discovery saturated the room as the energy entrainment built.[1] I encouraged the one who was loathe to

---

[1] *Entrainment is a basic law of physics—powerful rhythmic vibrations from one source will cause less powerful vibrations of another source to lock into the vibration of the first source.*

go near the ankle to beam energy at her from across the room. Some glanced up for reassurance and moved in close. The group energy increased, giving them the courage to experiment with their new-found talents.

Lorna moved in confidently, totally exhilarated by the process. Following my guidance, she drew in more and more healing energy. "I feel intense energy building in my hands," she exclaimed, "but something doesn't make sense. I'm almost sick from smelling a very strong, unpleasant odor." She shook her head, totally mystified. Those disgusting smells couldn't be coming from that elegant, immaculate redhead. "This is so strange. Doesn't anybody else smell it?" she asked. Heads shaking in unison confused her even more.

The class was unfolding organically. Lorna had just described a perfect example of an "extra-sensory" ability.

"Only people with clairsalience can smell non-physical odors," I grinned. "It means clear smelling. I've found that peculiar ability quite handy in diagnosis. For example, a very strong urine smell is often an indicator of bladder and kidney problems or gout. In this case, I suspect the toxins stored in Monique's bruised and swollen tissues are being released. You smell it because you have that gift."

Lorna proudly added clairsalience to her so-called normal senses.

As each person took a turn sending energy to Monique, she glowed radiantly and thanked them. They had no idea how fortunate they were to have so cooperative and receptive a subject for their first healing experience. I knew first hand that many people are not accustomed to receiving energy. I took a deep breath and faced the issue.

"It isn't always this easy. Sometimes clients will resist the healing process, even if they requested it," I began. Blank stares. "Sending energy to a person who isn't comfortable receiving it is as futile as trying to fill a glass when it's upside down. Even if it's unconscious, resistance prevents healing. This is a partnership. Unlike medical doctors, we don't fix people. After we provide energy, it's the client's job to use that energy to heal. The only permanent healing is self-healing."

A happy buzz filled the room as they eagerly described their personal sensations. The differences in subjective experience are always fascinating.

"It's amazing, but how does it work?" someone asked.

"Do you know how your television works?" I challenged. "You just turn it on and you get pictures, right? You don't have to know how the dots make pictures to watch TV. If you try to count the dots you can't enjoy the program. When you're in healing mode," I continued, "there's no room for doubt or analysis… no time to wonder how it's happening or whether it's working or not.

"I try my best not to second-guess God. All I know is that everything is created from energy and everything runs on energy. We use that energy every day to build, move and repair our bodies. It just never occurs to us that we're doing it. The more efficiently we work with the energy, the better the results. How does it work? It just works!"

Heads nodded as that sank in. They sat silently enjoying their instant comprehension and mutual understanding.

Intimations of Things to Come

It felt like the perfect time to end the class. "Nothing like ending on a happy note," I thought to myself.

Bernice suddenly broke the silence. "Hey, wait a minute, I have a chronic neck problem. How about working on that? After all, I did donate my apartment."

Again, heads nodded synchronously. Everyone agreed she was entitled to a healing.

"Okay," I sighed, "let's get you into the hot seat," and moved a chair to the center of the room.

She sat uneasily, not quite sure what she'd gotten herself into. Nevertheless, she was determined to get a free healing.

Lorna took a deep breath and chimed in, "Could I try to do the healing?"

"That's a great idea," I responded. "It'll be good practice for you. Take a moment to reconnect with the universal energy."

"Okay, like we did before?" she murmured.

"Right! Pull it down, let it flow through you and mingle with your own energy, then send it out toward Bernice."

Following my guidance, she stood confidently in front of Bernice and began beaming energy.

I positioned myself behind the chair, reinforcing Lorna's energy. "This is an advanced technique called a dyad," I explained, so the class could learn about this powerful healing method. "The energy is multiplied when two people focus on the same objective.

The energy did just that, but instead of relaxing into the usual state of peaceful wellbeing, Bernice became nervous and agitated. To calm and reassure her, I placed my hands on her forehead and neck. Suddenly her head jerked sideways violently.

"I feel like my neck just got cut off from my body!" she choked hysterically.

The image of a shining blade came crashing down toward me. That psychic flash told me exactly what had happened. As usual, the answer popped out unbidden. "Looks like you got on the wrong side of a guillotine," I blurted.

Bernice was scared and suspicious. "I want to know why this is happening to me!" she demanded. "When you were working on that other woman it wasn't anything like this!"

I explained that every healing is unique… different people, different conditions and different needs. "It might be helpful to integrate this experience into your present life," I suggested.

"Not acceptable!" she spat out angrily.

I offered to work with her privately in exchange for the use of her apartment.

"No thanks, I think I've had enough," she snapped, then turned on her heel and began tidying the room.

Lorna was in need of reassurance. I hurried over to her and whispered, "Good job. We'll talk about it later."

Bernice's roommate arrived and she rushed us out. All the way down the stairs I sent out prayers to Spirit to help me turn this into a positive lesson.

Out on the sidewalk silent stares begged an explanation. "This is a perfect example of the upside down glass," my mouth assured them. "You can't pour anything into it."

"Right!" Lorna grinned, then opened her arms wide for a group hug.

The trip home was plagued with doubts. Had Bernice's negative reaction offset the positive aspects of the class? Odds were she wouldn't allow us to use her apartment again. In that case, even if it was a go we'd have no place to meet.

It occurred to me that future classes, if any, would pale by comparison to such a stellar beginning. How could I live up to such high expectations? Sleep did not come easily.

The next day Lorna called with mixed reviews. "Everyone was amazed at Monique's healing but disturbed about what happened to Bernice. Some wondered if healing could actually be dangerous."

"That is the very thought that kept me awake last night," I responded.

"They were wondering what had happened. That woman was shaking all over when she felt her head being chopped off," she said, "but I reminded them about the upside down glass. Is there anything else I could have said?"

"No, that was perfect!" I assured her. "It's a shame she wouldn't let me work it through with her. I have no slick answer for what came through. We'll just deal with any concerns in the next class."

No one was surprised when Bernice came up with a flimsy excuse as to why we couldn't use the space for week two. As I had feared, we were a class without a home.

When my mentor heard of our dilemma he kindly offered the use of his living room. We couldn't have had a better spot for our second class. It looked like a go.

Alex's unexpected generosity kept the class going. One small miracle after another confirmed that we were on the right track, doing something needed and valuable. Thus encouraged, I asked Kitty, a private client, if she would be willing to volunteer for a class of fledgling healers. She was thrilled to get a free treatment.

The class had grown, in numbers and enthusiasm. What a relief! Members of the first class filled the newcomers in on the principles they'd learned and encouraged them to join in. The dreaded questions about Monique's reaction were never asked.

We were off to a flying start with the class beaming energy at Kitty while I worked on the colitis that had plagued her for years. Kitty's face and posture registered a very positive healing experience. Everyone was thoroughly enjoying themselves. Healing tends to bring out the best in everyone.

Bye Bye Bad Karma

Spiritual Midwifery

As the healing session wound down, Lorna frantically signaled for help. When I rushed to comfort her she whispered that since the healing began, she'd been feeling really weird.

My student was in trouble, and it sounded serious. "I keep getting these strange flashes of myself with knees up in the air and blood all over the place," she mumbled. "It's me, but it isn't. Is it possible that I died during childbirth in another incarnation?"

Instinctively, I placed my hands on her forehead and crown chakras and aimed healing energy at her full blast. In crisis mode, I sent out a silent prayer for guidance.

In a barely audible choked whisper, she murmured, "I've lost my feet!"

"How can you lose your feet," I blurted.

"I don't know," she gulped, "I can't feel them. It's like they're not even there."

I motioned for help and we dragged her across the room and laid her on a couch. I dropped to my knees and held her in a feeble attempt at comfort. Fighting panic with the voice in my head predicting dire consequences, I focused on healing.

A restless stirring in the class registered vaguely, but the healing energy somehow reassured them.

Lorna's distress was getting worse by the minute. Powerful rhythmic contractions began, lifting her head and shoulders off the couch. In shock and disbelief, she blurted, "I'm 28 years old and I've never been pregnant, but I'm in labor!" Her pancake-flat stomach distended so much it looked as if a basketball had been placed under her loose dress.

We were right there with her… all of us. Lorna's false labor was so real that two women leaped up, grabbed her hands and shouted, "Push! Push!" Vivian, a fellow med student, curled up at her feet in fetal position and clung to her dress.

My student was in trouble! Something had to be done… now… but what? Beyond helpless, I did the only thing I could. A silent scream erupted from the depth of my being, "God… somebody… help!"

A peculiar calm enveloped me and a warm, loving presence flooded me with peace, power and wisdom. Until that moment I firmly believed a Spirit could not enter a sane person's body, but this was way too real to deny.

With perfect ease, confidence and control, my hands reached out, beaming energy and comfort to Lorna. Then my mouth began asking incredibly wise, insightful questions. The logical part of my brain was a stunned observer, fascinated by the brilliance flowing through me.

I was in shock, but everything proceeded rather well without me. I watched the scene and listened to what was said in an odd state of dual consciousness. It felt as if I was lip-synching the words of a master psychologist (Jung, maybe). I struggled to project a semblance of confidence to the class. They were mesmerized.

I listened as the unfamiliar voice coming out of my mouth asked compellingly urgent questions. The voice asked Lorna how she was feeling. Lorna responded with clinical precision: "The labor has been so prolonged and the bleeding so profuse that there's less and less blood for the heart to circulate. The heart is struggling, but there's just not enough blood left to pump to the extremities. That's why there's no feeling in them."

"How ironic," I thought, "This 20th century student is doing a medical critique of a death scene in the 17th century." Academic studies and scientific principles couldn't possibly explain it. This was a first-hand glimpse into an all-too-common human drama from the past.

Spirit (the only way I could describe the gentle-strong presence that had taken me over) amended the query: "How are you feeling emotionally?"

"Oh!" she responded, "Well, I can't explain it, but there's this feeling of tremendous anger."

"What are you angry about? Are you angry at the unborn child that's causing you such terrible pain?"

It was such a logical line of questioning that I relaxed, knowing we were in good hands.

Lorna's head shook violently. "No, no, no!"

"Are you angry at the people who are helping you?"

She spat out a contemptuous, "No! Of course not! They're doing their best."

"Then what is causing you to be so angry?"

"I don't know, but it's a cold fury. I'm angry enough to kill." Her fingers curled into such hard fists that the nails bit deeply into her palms. With sudden unquestioning certainty, a flat statement shot out of me, "The bastard didn't show up, did he?" I was appalled by what had just come out of my mouth.

Her jaw dropped in an involuntary gasp that signaled a direct hit. I consciously forced my body to relax. That could explain why she was so angry. As a female and mother, I could relate. How could anything be more infuriating? There she was, in agony, bleeding to death having his baby and this guy didn't even show up!

"Where is this man?" I wondered. A second later I was flying in midair over a dense forest, a search party of one. More panic and a rapid-fire barrage of questions washed over me. "Where am I? How did I get here? How will I get back? How can I even recognize the guy if I find him?"

With a sudden, sickening lurch, I jerked to a halt in midair. Compelled by curiosity, I looked down and there it was… a bloody body thrown loose-jointed like a rag doll at the edge of a trail. In less than a breath-span I was back in the dimly-lit primitive room calmly relating what I had seen.

"Your husband did not ignore you or desert you," I blurted. "He's not out fooling around or playing cards with the boys. The only reason he's not here with you is that he was waylaid by a bunch of Indians." No amount of inner turmoil, doubts, reluctance, or confusion could prevent me from delivering that message.

The deathly pale woman on the blood-soaked bed grimaced with yet another contraction. "Yeah, sure!" came her icy response. Fury unabated, she was having none of it. "I'm dying… alone. I know it… and my husband is not here!"

"If you don't believe us, just go and see for yourself!" my Spirit ventriloquist challenged.

"How do I do that?" she shot back belligerently.

Oh, so calmly, my altered voice intoned, "Simply float out of your body, through the ceiling, through the roof. Then ask to be taken to your husband and you'll go there automatically."

"Very well, I'll try," she answered tersely.

The silence was deafening. Everyone in the room held their breath. Every second felt like forever.

The anger melted away; her body relaxed and she announced calmly, "I'm ready to go now."

"Ready to go where?" I burst out, unable to remain silent any longer. "Ready to go find your husband?"

"No. I'm ready to go… now!" the woman announced firmly.

Lorna's own voice came through in a plaintive whisper, "Does this mean I'm going to die?"

That question echoed through the room loud and clear. It was all I could do to keep the energy flowing.

Spirit's blithe reassurance relieved us all. "Not you, dear… her. By forgiving her husband she has freed herself, and you, of karma. This is occurring on a consciousness level only. You are more than fine. Relax."

Lorna settled peacefully to follow the guidance. Despite my jagged breathing, the disembodied Spirit voice continued, serene and loving. "Float upward, away from your body just as you did before. This time keep going, beyond the roof, past the trees and the mountains, then onward to the edge of the Earth's atmosphere. See the beautiful lights streaking toward you? Those are loving spirits coming from afar to escort you into the next phase of your being. Trust them!"

A beautiful smile transformed Lorna's face. The tension in the room dissolved into a communal sigh of relief that everything was okay. In that one moment death was redefined from "the end" to a new beginning.

Halfway between suspension and expansion of reality, I felt their growing response to the phenomenon that had just occurred. Whispered speculations about the deeper complex meanings of the miracle they'd been privileged to witness filled the room.

Almost as if by magic, a serenely smiling Lorna was back with us.

Everyone was beyond impatient to hear every last detail. "What happened?" they pleaded. "Why did you decide to go?"

"Well, when I followed the instructions to float through the roof and look for the husband," she began. "I hung around on the ceiling for a minute looking at the body on the bed and the people in the room."

"What people?" the class erupted in unison.

"Oh, there was a woman, maybe two, a toddler and I think a baby. Anyway, I kept on floating through the ceiling till I was above the roof. Then, out of curiosity, I looked down and discovered I was above a log cabin. I… she… thought about it and decided it wasn't really necessary to see a bloody body. I realized it was probably true that he was set upon by Indians and slipped back into the room.

"After we forgave her husband, I felt my job was done and it was time to get out of there. The rest," she twinkled at us, "was one of the easiest things I've ever done. Once convinced the me I am today was not dying, leaving the body was a lovely, very gentle experience for both of us."

The effect on the class was magical. The angst of witnessing death by proxy was transmuted into eternal wisdom. Spiritually and emotionally they'd travelled light years together.

Without a clue as to how to proceed, I settled for logistics. "Before we go we must decide on a place to meet. We can't impose upon Alex's kindness indefinitely."

Bobbi, a petite dancer, volunteered her apartment. There went a perfectly acceptable graceful exit. With a pang of regret, I accepted her generosity—and my fate

One by one, class members tore themselves away and headed back into their ordinary lives. Something had shifted within each of us. Some were thoughtful, others filled with elation that bubbled through them like champagne.

Disorientation Squared

No one should ride a New York City subway at midnight in such a state. Cataclysmic events or no, I had to get home. Once away from the glow of excitement generated by the class, I crashed. Dazed and disoriented, I barely made it onto the train. Nothing seemed to make sense.

How easily everything could have gone wrong. Thank God it didn't, but was it really a miracle? What if Lorna, in her eagerness to become a healer, had fantasized it all? Instant rejection! It was far too real! The basketball-sized bulge under her dress that had appeared out of nowhere and vanished like magic was no delusion. That physical manifestation couldn't be wished away.

Then there were the startling aspects of the regression itself. According to authorities on reincarnation, and traditional wisdom as well, "the past" cannot be changed. And how about the concept of giving new information to "past incarnations?" Yet Spirit had spoken directly to that woman and instructed her to leave her body and confront the truth about her husband. That 17th century pioneer woman dying in childbirth grudgingly followed instructions and had an epiphany. Then, based on information Spirit provided, she forgave her husband and serenely chose to "go." Her change of heart and spiritual growth validated Spirit's approach and changed reality for all of us. Mind-boggling!

Ruminations and Ramifications

My brain felt like a bag of over-stretched rubber bands. I meticulously reviewed the disconnected thoughts ricocheting in my head like images in a shattered mirror. The 17th century woman and Spirit had been as vividly real as anyone in the room. Every single person in that class was totally convinced that Lorna had actually:

(a) Merged with a colonial woman dying of childbirth gone wrong.
(b) Floated above her roof.
(c) Been convinced the woman's husband had been killed by Indians.
(d) Helped her forgive him for not being there when she was dying, giving birth to their child.

After the woman forgave her husband it seemed perfectly logical for Spirit to help her "leave her body" and call upon beings from the spirit world to escort her into a wonderful new life. Extraordinary!

Exhausted mentally and physically, I crawled into bed and drifted to sleep thanking God for the privilege of witnessing that once-in-a-lifetime miracle. However, it hadn't changed my opinion about past life regression. One isolated event could be written off as an aberration, right?

Despite attempts to downplay the incident, reasoning fell flat. The next few days were haunted by the memory of the wise spirit presence that put me on like a glove, and the poignant reality of the colonial woman's suffering. Words, phrases and images from the drama kept intruding into whatever I was doing. As real as it had seemed at the time, more doubts and questions were raised than answered.

The 800-pound gorilla in the room was reincarnation. I'd always been turned off by the traditional Indian wheel of life cycles of transmigration. It was revolting to think rats (ugh!) were worshipped as ancestors. Suffering through animal and human incarnations in restitution for past sins was my idea of cruel and unusual punishment. Further, the final reward after all that torture… nothingness, the eternal bliss of Nirvana… hardly seemed worth the effort. Nonetheless, I accepted some form of reincarnation as an intrinsic part of the immortal human spirit.

Vivid flashbacks precluded total rejection of the concept. I was three years old sitting on the floor struggling to learn to tie my shoelaces. After many failures, a visitor from some distant point in time landed in front of me. At first I thought it might be an angel, but this fellow was nothing like the ones in the Bible stories my Grandmother read to me. Instead of wings and flowing robes, he wore a shiny blue suit with short pants and long socks.[2] His light brown hair was long and curly like a woman's. There was fancy white lace at his throat and wrists and every finger sparkled with big shiny rings. This was fascinating. The only rings I'd ever seen were plain gold wedding bands.

The mystery man stared at me with total contempt. "With that stupid brain and those clumsy fingers, how can they expect me to do anything?" he sputtered. I was spellbound. Everybody would laugh at me if I told them about him, but it was so real it replayed over and over in my head. "Where did he come from and why was he so mad?" I wondered. By the age of five I had come to the conclusion that the man in the blue suit was somebody I used to be. I just knew he had been born rich and very, very smart but had wasted his chance to do a big, important job. Waste was bad! I decided that God turned him into a little girl in the Depression to teach him a lesson. Things like that happened in the Bible, according to Grandma.

---

[2] *Years later I was stunned to find an exact illustration of that outfit in a history book. The fashion was popular in the court of Louis XV!*

Mary Blake

As time passed the intensity of the memory faded. It was easier to think of it as childhood fantasy rather than reality. There were no more encounters with other incarnations (unless you count the strange guests at my tea parties). In 1978, while visiting the ruins of Machu Picchu, I glimpsed two Peruvian incarnations, one male and one female.

The following year, an astral projection class transported me to a deserted country road. I was walking beside a cart with a squeaky wheel. The wheat in the field beside the road was ripe and ready for harvesting, but it was way too short. That told me this was a long time ago. A tiny church steeple in the distance was the only sign of civilization. There were no further clues as to when this was or where I was. That brief astral trip whetted my appetite to explore the past.

Later that year, while studying in London, I attended lectures and classes at the Spiritualist Association of Great Britain. It seemed the perfect time to see if I could track down that arrogant French nobleman. I asked the Director of the SAGB for a recommendation to a highly respected past life regressionist and made an appointment. A friend offered to accompany me. The endeavor didn't start off well at all. The regressionist was unable to hypnotize me.

Undaunted, I suggested we try again. Without informing him, I decided to employ the astral projection technique that had taken me to that lonely dirt road. It worked just fine. I connected with a lighthearted male Cathari healer returning from a successful herb gathering trip in the woods. A moment later he was frozen in horror, watching his entire community burn to the ground. He had arrived too late to prevent everyone, including his own wife and baby, from being burned alive.

"That poor man!" my friend moaned. "He lost everything and everyone he cared for." At her request, we shifted forward within that lifetime and there I was, a very old man squatting in the woods. My beard grazed the ground. It was near the end of a hermetic life spent hiding in the woods to avoid religious fanatics. Without knowing how or why, I knew it was 12th century France.

The regressionist, unaware that I was not under his control, assumed I was an Anchorite. He expounded endlessly on his extensive knowledge of their treatment in 14th century England. The old man responded calmly, "You may call me anything you like, young man." It really didn't matter to him that the regressionist was describing a different country and a different century.

I suspected he was trying to impress my blonde girlfriend with his brilliance. Penny, unimpressed, insisted that she wanted to hear the wisdom of this ancient healer.

It was annoying that the "past life" he described was totally different from the man I had connected with. Obviously, he was indulging in a pet fantasy or making it up out of whole cloth. That failed experiment convinced me that past life regression was a hoax.

Now, faced with compelling new evidence, I realized a drastic reevaluation of that opinion was in order. To be fair, one botched attempt was pretty flimsy evidence to prove that all regressions were fraudulent. I made that trip to the 12th century on my own, without hypnosis. Lorna's spontaneous non-hypnotic regression was witnessed by a room full of rational people. Was that enough to tip the scale? I finally decided to stop trying to make sense of circumstances beyond my comprehension and get a decent night's sleep.

Chapter Two
Super Class?

The next class started off on a happy note. We connected with the universal healing energy and dedicated the class to positive, loving healing of ourselves and the planet. After the opening ritual I asked for comments, questions and benefits gained from the classes so far.

That sparked a lively discussion about the positive effects in their daily lives that they attributed to the class work. Everyone had something special to report. Collectively we gave thanks for the miracles that were happening in our lives. New members listened wide-eyed with wonder that so much had occurred in such a short time.

In that grateful mood, I addressed the many forms and definitions of energy, both ancient and modern. I started with a brief description of *prana*, the Sanskrit word meaning "life force" or "vital principle that comprises all cosmic energy permeating the Universe." Next came a description of *chi*, the energy source in Chinese traditional medicine. Charts of the two systems revealed that they were very similar.

Heads nodded as I suggested it was beyond coincidence that so many ancient cultures had arrived independently at an energy system long ridiculed by modern medicine. I cited recent laboratory experiments that had (finally) proven scientifically that such an energy system exists. Everyone was amazed that ancient acupuncture meridians corresponded almost exactly with the major ganglia of Western medicine.

That led neatly into a discussion of chakras and how they receive, store and generate energy. Some were already aware of the seven major chakras within the body and their connection to our daily lives. I described the importance of the flow of energy throughout the body and how accidents and emotional shocks can cause blockages that affect health, happiness and creativity. Finally, we progressed to colors and sounds that play such a vital part in traditional healing.

I assured them these invisible energies are real, not magical. Similar to electricity, that energy might as well not be there unless you know how to harness it. By this time my students were eager to discover how to tap into this energy and use it. I proposed a simple exercise… to beam colors at a class volunteer. The room was filled with excitement as they prepared to bombard a class member with color.

Vivian volunteered to be our healing subject for the evening. As a medical student, she was intrigued by the discussion of energy. "Besides, I could really use a healing," she smiled.

She lay on the couch in full view of the class, gratefully absorbing the colorful healing energy beamed at her. Suddenly everything spun out of control… again. As in the first two classes, we were propelled into a realm of miracles that surpassed all expectation.

In one sudden movement Vivian's body flipped over like a rag doll thrown face down. "Old-timers" from the first two classes exchanged knowing glances.

"Here we go again," someone murmured.

Fighting panic, I sent up desperate petitions for help and put every ounce of strength I had into beaming healing energy at Vivian.

"How did her body manage to do that?" someone murmured, echoing my own thoughts.

From Africa in Chains

After the convulsive flop onto her stomach, her head began to beat rhythmically against the couch. From all appearances, she was paralyzed from the neck down.

Nervous energy swept through the room. Newcomers gaped helplessly, jaws unhinged. Initiates reached out to reassure them that Spirit would keep her safe.

Lorna was on her feet, sniffing some intense odor no one else could smell. To my immense relief, Spirit arrived immediately, assumed command, offered comfort and gently asked, "What is your name?"

Unintelligible murmurs between head bumps did nothing to ease the tension.

"Tell us where you are… in English, please," Spirit requested.

"Far from home," came the brusque reply, in a voice so deep and foreign some gasped in shock.

"Where is home?" Spirit prompted gently.

"Home… just home."

"What is happening to you?"

"Hard things tie me to wood," came the hoarse reply.

"Chains!" someone whispered.

"What can you see?" Spirit asked.

"What an odd question to ask someone who was banging her head against the couch, I thought, then chided myself, "Spirit always asks the right questions. Stop second guessing and let Spirit run things."

"Boards… grey wood boards. A floor," he gasped.

"What else can you see?"

"Door. White man come through door, throw food at us. Go."

"What country are you in?"

"No country. Homeland far away… we travel far over big water."

"Where?" Silence. "What water?"

A grunt.

Patiently, Spirit probed for the information needed to help this person. The answers came in a hoarse masculine voice.

Lorna stood tall and strong, aiming a steady stream of healing energy toward her friend. Her face first registered confusion, then concern, as her psychic talent told her what was happening.

Once more I listened passively, fascinated at Spirit's remarkably astute questions issuing through my mouth.

"What was life like before you came here?" Spirit asked.

"My father, Chief of Chiefs, taught me how to rule, be strong, be fair… be good leader." His face altered at the warm remembrance of a good life.

"Prince and heir," I thought to myself. "He must have felt the jungle was his private kingdom."

"Bad men catch me in jungle," he blurted. "I trapped by hunters of men. Enemy tribe work with bad white men."

"Slave traders!" a class member whispered.

"They tie me like animal with thongs and vines, then jerk me… drag me places I don't know… days… far…"

"You alone?"

"No, many others, some strangers, some my people. They beat slow ones. We go many days to big, big water—nothing but water and strange house on water. They herd us like animals down dark hole and fasten us to floor with hard things, not vines, not thongs. Hurt bad when try to move."

Everyone was deeply affected by this intimate glimpse of the appalling, inhumane treatment of the helpless captives. Tears trickled unbidden down cheeks. Some reached for the nearest hand for comfort. Never before had any of us felt so deeply connected with a slave.

The innate decency and sensitivity of this jungle prince was starkly revealed by his description of the suffering and agonizing deaths of his fellow captives. Shackled to rings in the floor, he saw very little but felt much. Crying babies clung desperately to dead mothers. Death and the stench of it… terror and heartbreak were everywhere, every day.

Lorna retched so convulsively she almost lost her balance. Clairsalience has its disadvantages.

Choking back a sob, the African described the bestial behavior of his captors. "They drag the dead and almost dead across the holding deck and throw them into the sea. I live. Maybe one in four of 'the cargo' they call us, still here."

The ship docked in the American colonies. The surviving cargo was driven ashore, herded like animals to a public square and lined up on a platform. The class was frozen with horror at the graphic description of a slave auction.

To Be Sold & Let

"Bad, more bad, all bad," he cried. "I see young girl, not yet woman… daughter of friend. She tremble like leaf in rainstorm; cry out… hurt, shamed. I push white man hurting her away… Aeeih! Hurt bad!"

"What happened?" several class members gasped.

Spirit quietly addressed the class in sober tones. "That act of quixotic bravery, an aborted attempt to defend the modesty of a child from his village, infuriated his new master."

Next came the last thing any one of us wanted to hear.

"White man beat me…" he gasped, confirming the accuracy of

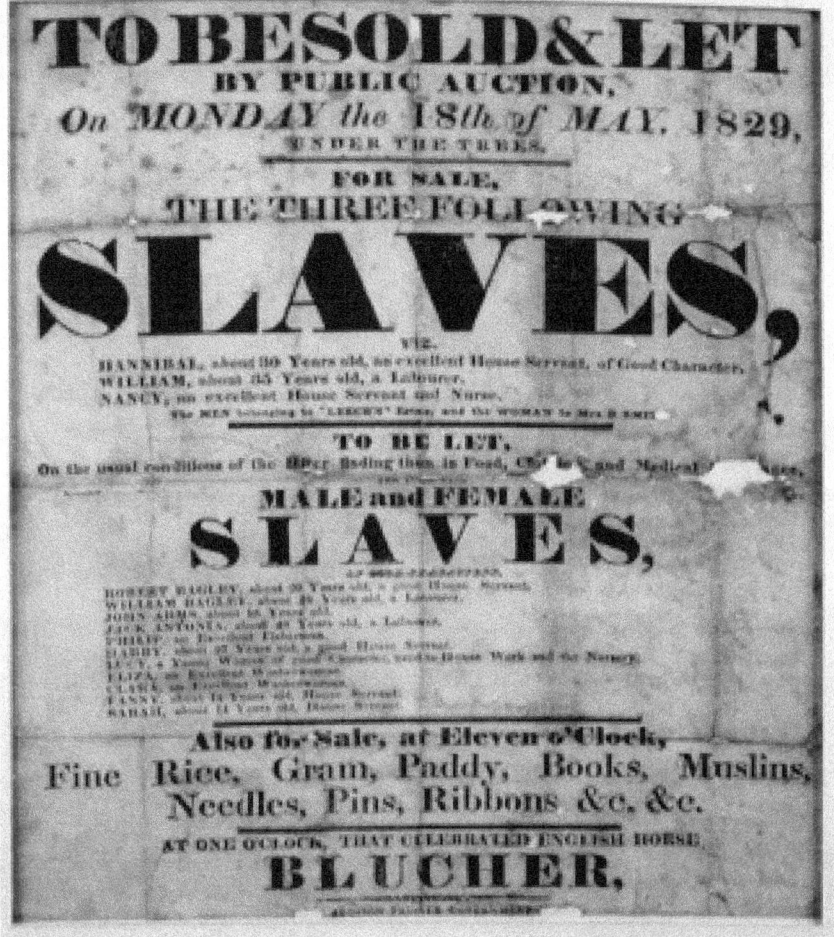

Spirit's explanation. "Cut me so I no can run… no can fight… hard to walk."

Heads nodded sadly as they realized he was deliberately mutilated to prevent attempts to escape.

His matter-of-fact description of the years that followed grew more and more bleak and bitter. His birthright, that glowing future, had been abruptly canceled. "Many hard years of slave life and then I got sick and died."

"What happened that caused you to die?" blurted a class member.

"White people say it consumption."

Spirit personally escorted the African's emancipated spirit on a peaceful journey into a happier place in the hereafter. He was gone and Vivian was back. A roomful of students beamed love and healing at her with all they had in them.

In the void left by the African's departure, the class was restless and deeply moved.

"You just participated in a metaphysical rebirthing," Spirit announced. "Your energy and your caring helped this miracle to happen. You have had the rare privilege of assisting an exploited, tortured noble soul to leave that pain-wracked body and ascend into its proper place in the cosmos with dignity and confidence." That said, he was gone.

Filled with pride and compassion, we drew in our first full, deep communal breath since the African had appeared.

Back with us, Vivian needed no coaxing to share her intimate insights into the soul-wrenching experience. It was all there, vivid and intense as if it had actually happened to her. The class was enthralled by her description of the places and people she had seen. They wanted to know how the African felt about everything. She was most impressed with the nobility, the gentle power, and stoic courage of this remarkable person.

The Consumption Connection

I noticed a subtle change in affect and the timbre of her voice. Someone commented that she didn't appear to be as frail as she had seemed earlier in the evening.

"But what could you possibly have in common with that African slave?" someone asked,

She stopped and took a deep breath before answering. "This is something I've never, ever revealed in public. When I was 17 I was diagnosed with tuberculosis. Whoever heard of contracting TB in the sixties in an exclusive Chicago suburb? The chances against it are astronomical! Can you imagine the implications, the significance of this," she crowed. "That African man died of consumption!"

The consumption connection was not lost on the class. Most of us knew it was a common name for tuberculosis. No one doubted this evidence of Spirit in action, in a scenario beyond their wildest imagination. A newcomer asked Lorna, "What was all that sniffing and retching about?"

"Oh, that's my special psychic gift," she smiled. "And the funniest thing, I knew exactly what I was smelling. It was the powerful musky smell of a black man under intense emotional pressure. I was just thinking that it might come in handy as a doctor. This was the first time I've deliberately used my new… or maybe old, but decidedly unique… diagnostic technique. Hmm."

Once again, the class had spiraled far off course from my agenda. It assumed a life of its own and traveled through time to heal a wounded spirit.

A special kinship shone bright on every face as they hugged long and hard, then reluctantly headed home.

Decompression

Despite the group's exuberant response, I was as disoriented as a deep-sea diver in need of decompression. The pressure of leading a class without a clue as to what was happening was wearing. With a strange sense of déjà vu, I sank onto a subway seat, grateful that the car was nearly empty. I wondered if the inner turmoil showed on my face. "Ah, so what," I reflected. "These are New Yorkers. They're used to all kinds of weirdos." That inside joke settled me a bit.

Gratitude and awe-filled humility aside, these illogical miracles were profoundly unsettling. Why were these amazing things happening in my healing class? Maybe the combined energy of the group tuning in to the universal healing energy and focusing their energy on one subject had accidentally triggered the process. Who knew?

Once-in-a-lifetime events just don't happen in pairs. This couldn't be brushed off as mere chance. For a medical student who'd never been pregnant to connect with a lifetime in which she died in childbirth was remarkable. A second regression, to a lifetime as an African slave who died from consumption, by a young TB victim from an affluent Chicago suburb, was beyond coincidence. My logical mind searched for a spiritual principle to describe how it worked.

One reassuring consolation soothed my torment. Twice we'd been flung headlong into unknown dimensions from which we had returned whole, safe, and somehow the better for it. I fell asleep still trying to sort out the deep spiritual meaning of it all.

Salutary Repercussions

The next class began with the sweetest music a healer could possibly hear. Lorna burst into the class almost exploding with excitement. Drawing me aside she whispered, "I've got to tell you about my miracle! It's unbelievable and it's all because of what happened with that colonial woman who died in childbirth!"

"Fantastic! I'm thrilled, but let's wait till everyone's here." I suggested. "After we do our clearing and focusing, the floor is yours. If it's that good I want the whole class to hear it."

We breathed out the tensions of the day, freed ourselves of negative emotions and drew in the healing energy as usual. When we were harmoniously attuned I announced Lorna had something special to tell us. I was as eager as everyone else to hear her news.

With pure joy, Lorna announced, "A miracle happened! Because of my experience in our second class, I just had the most wonderful menstrual period of my life—no pain! Every single month I have been going through pure hell. I have been in bed for days. The torture was so severe I spent half the time between menses dreading the next one. I was walking along and was shocked to realize my period was actually beginning without warning. It was just a normal flow instead of two days of agonizing pain. Nothing else has changed, so it has to be because of my incarnation as a pioneer woman who died in childbirth.

"The best explanation I have is that if one had bled to death from a particular orifice, bleeding from that area could trigger unconscious fear… Each month my body would tense up tight as a drum. It's cause and effect! Muscle tension can cause painful menstruation. Now I know the real reason I've suffered such agony all my life. Oh, and another thing—I've always been afraid of dying. Not any more!"

That brought a round of applause. The room hummed with enthusiastic discussions about unlimited potential benefits of visits to other lifetimes. They were amazed at the dual healing that freed the colonial woman and ended the trail of resentment and pain that had plagued Lorna all her life.

Vivian, too, reported positive benefits. She raved about how uncommonly well, confident and energetic she felt. She traced her increased wellbeing directly to the noble African slave's release from a life of affliction and degradation. She couldn't stop smiling.

After such heartwarming news, I looked forward to a nice, normal healing class. The topic was meditation. Starting with a brief outline of the history, traditions and value of the process, I moved on to cover some of the mental, physical and emotional advantages of meditation. I outlined some of the reasons beginners find it difficult to reach a meditative state. We spent some time with yoga breathing and practicing a technique to control the "gerbil thoughts" that bushwhack the beginner.

After practicing a bit, someone asked if I would help them go deeper into a meditative state. The class was enthusiastic, as usual, but two of the individual meditations were anything but usual. In rapid succession, they each took off on what I was beginning to think of as soul travel.

Nothing could have pleased me less. Way beyond the edge of my comfort zone, I managed to hide my relief each time they came back in one piece. To me, these unexplained paranormal phenomena were downright scary. I had begun these classes firmly convinced "past life regression" was either fraud, self-delusion or a combination of both. How or why my students kept embarking upon these unsettling adventures was a mystery. Perhaps the intense energy the class generated could trigger spontaneous spiritual combustion. Whatever activated it, this cosmic crash course I'd blundered onto hurtled on at warp speed.

As we hugged goodnight Darren, a psychologist working with the New York City Board of Mental Health, invited me for coffee. As we settled into the booth I asked, "Okay, Darren, what's up?"

"I really want to experience a trip into another lifetime," he confided, "but not in public. For professional and personal reasons, it just wouldn't work. Could we please make an appointment to do this privately?" His eyes emphasized the seriousness of his request.

"Look, Darren, I have no idea what forces might be in play here. I've never seen any spontaneous trips into other lifetimes before."

He nodded thoughtfully, "I've never run across anything like this in my advanced professional studies or in anything I've ever read… and I've read a lot!"

"Yeah, it's a mystery. I've puzzled over it ever since it started, and all I can think is it might be the class energy. If that's the case a private session might not work. How can I guarantee results?"

Darren smiled reassuringly, "I'm willing to risk failure if you are."

"Okay, let's consider it an experiment that could go either way."

With that understanding, we set the appointment.

Inner Doubts and Deliberations

Once again, I rode the subway in deep turmoil. The mind games playing out in my head were new, yet oddly familiar. As one who identified with Robert A. Heinlein's novel *Stranger in a Strange Land*, it should have been easier. I agonized about preparations for the coming ordeal. Sorting clues from the other four "trips," and analyzing every detail might be a good way to start.

The prospect of working with a trained psychologist triggered major self-doubts. It would help if I knew how it happened. There was no reference to interactions with other incarnations anywhere in the books on reincarnation. My one slim hope was that the unseen Spirit who had taken the reins in class would take pity on me and help. But was that even possible outside the class?

The events were so overwhelming that real breakthroughs slipped by almost unnoticed. I had barely acknowledged the fact that our uncontrived trips to other lifetimes had all generated positive results. Some professional I was!

Our solo venture would require a leap of faith for both of us. What if nothing happened? All four events that occurred in class were extemporaneous, with no prompting or direction from me. All I did was call for help when things got out of hand.

The possibility of success was more unsettling than the prospect of failure. At least Darren had assured me that failure would be okay with him.

Chapter Three
First Solo Flight

Onward into the fire I rode on my trusty subway. The trip to Manhattan was fraught with misgivings interlaced with internal pep talks. Relying on "spontaneous regressions" from the class was no help at all. My skills had nothing to do with those events. All I could do was show up, "let go and let God." From then on it would be up to Spirit... or not.

Darren greeted me warmly. We made a makeshift bed of pillows on the living room floor. I said a prayer, broadcast a silent plea for help and dove in. We began with the familiar relaxation technique we used in class. I silently offered myself as an instrument of Divine Purpose, drew in the universal healing energy and pleaded for Spirit to put the right words in my mouth. Thus committed, the confidence and expertise I dared not hope for manifested automatically.

The seasoned professional analyst followed my guidance with faith borne of witnessing four spontaneous regressions. He was much more confident than I. Tailor-made guided imagery floated him gently into altered consciousness. For a few moments, the only sound in the room was his gentle, shallow breathing. I wondered if he had simply fallen asleep and would eventually waken to the humiliating failure I fully expected.

I heard my voice instructing him to go to another time, another place, another aspect of himself that was experiencing something important for him to know about and deal with. It seemed such a daunting task I held my breath.

Contact!

A beat later the assured, mature psychologist was curled up into a small ball, sobbing quietly. I sent up a plea for help and focused on my job.

When I reached out to comfort the child, he quickly regained his dignity and stopped sobbing.

A small voice accustomed to command demanded, "Who are you? How dare you disturb me in my time of grief?"

My stunned silence made things worse. "Were you sent to spy upon me by my father's advisors? Can you not leave me a moment of privacy?" he snapped. The affect and arrogance told me he was accustomed to having his own way. Apology and an offer to help was met with disbelief.

"I've come a long way to assist you in your time of grief," I explained hesitantly.

"If you're not from here, then you must be an enemy. Out!" he commanded, "I will not speak with one of the monsters who killed my father!"

I explained that we came from a different world.

"You're not from the jungle? How can that be?" the haughty child demanded.

"It's the truth. Please tell us what's happening," I responded.

"I'm preparing to go into danger alone to prove my manhood so I can take my father's place. I must do this."

Spirit arrived and calmly took over. "How old are you?"

"Old enough!" he snapped. "I'm almost seven."

Spirit introduced Darren as a member of the boy's spiritual family who had come from a faraway land, and asked how we could be of service.

"If you're not from here, how can you understand?" he asked.

Spirit calmly and logically outlined a process that would test the credulity of a twentieth century metaphysics student. "Ah, it's simple. You and Darren, your soul brother, can trade information so you can know what he knows and he can learn what you know. Just open your mind and let it happen."

I wondered how a primitive child could understand this.

Comprehension came almost instantly—his, not mine! Darren's normal voice broke through offering details: "According to the picture I see, this is between two large lands, with water all about. This must be the Central American jungle. I'm still not certain of the time frame."

A few more questions and answers clarified the situation. We had connected with the son of a chief who had been killed defending their city from an invading force. The battle was won, but the leader was lost. Now the boy was determined to prove himself capable of taking his father's place. As only son and heir, this responsibility took precedence over grief. With some pride, he declared that no one his age had ever attempted such a feat.

Then, addressing Darren privately, Spirit issued a challenge: "You are a professional. Your skill and training are needed here. Reach out to this young boy and help him through his ordeal. He needs you."

In my little corner of consciousness, I was totally lost. Spirit's next words filled in the blanks: "The beautiful light above you is your soul brother, Darren. He and I have come here to assist you. We will be with you constantly. No one but you will be able to see us. Please understand you may rely upon us for advice when you encounter difficulties, but the effort and the triumph will be yours alone."

My left hemisphere admired Spirit's diplomatic, delicately phrased approach. Fascinated, I relaxed and listened.

Puberty Ritual

Reluctantly, the child agreed to accept the offer. In a public ceremony, he accepted the list of challenges and the standard equipment—a stone knife and thongs—to carry him through the ordeal. Thus equipped, he trudged stoically into the jungle.

Nightfall taxed his courage. Sheltered and protected from birth, he needed all the support he could get. Though lacking in jungle experience, Darren was well equipped to deal with a frightened child confronting such danger. His training as a marathon runner added endurance skills to psychological expertise.

Teeth chattering from the cold, they finally found shelter in a cave. "I've never been alone before—ever, even for a moment," the child murmured, more to himself than to us.

"You're not alone," Darren assured him warmly, "we are here for you. We're on your side. We will stay with you."

I marveled at the ease with which Darren adapted to the task, speaking first in the voice of the child and then his own. It was amazing how easily he identified with this boy from another lifetime, another culture, another age.

Of necessity, the boy learned to trust and mastered the primitive skills required to meet the time-honored challenges of candidates twice his age. "I must not shame my father's memory," was his battle cry.

Jungle Legend

The jungle tests of courage and stamina were formidable. Many more mature candidates had not survived the ritual; some never overcame the shame of failure.

"Easy now," came Darren's gentle, encouraging prompts, "you can do it… try it another way."

Spirit's serene confidence and restraint helped those soul brothers bond in a remarkable time-shattering, cross-cultural partnership. With difficulty, I held back and let them do it on their own.

Mere survival was only part of the ordeal. He had to kill a dangerous wild animal more than twice his size and bring back the trophy. He also had to provide physical evidence of having conquered dangerous mountains, rivers and jungle traps. Against all odds, he gamely met the challenges head on. Each triumph strengthened his resolve. Fierce determination to prove himself fit to assume his father's place as chief was far greater than the peril.

Many days later, exhausted but triumphant, the boy returned with all the trophies and symbols required to prove his courage and be accepted into manhood. After passing every test with flying colors he was formally initiated as chief and given his new name.

Spiritual bonding with Darren seemed to have affected him far more deeply than the endurance tests. Spirit spun us forward into the young chief's future. I had a vague sense of life unfolding at an accelerated time-skimming rate that left me reeling. Throughout an unusually long reign as chief he instituted many humanitarian innovations previously unknown to his race. His name became legend.

As he returned from his voyage, Darren's eyes flickered open with a silent plea for time to disentangle himself from that other reality. I sat quietly at his side.

Phenomenal Results

In heavy-laden stillness, we made our separate ways back to some sense of reality. I beamed energy at Darren's quiescent form and thought about the regressions so far. I relived the wonder of Lorna's connection with the dying woman and the three successive trips into other lifetimes. Through a haze of perplexity, I faced doubt, denial and my futile attempts to understand what was happening.

A deep sigh and gentle stirring brought me sharply back to the job at hand. I reached for Darren's hand, as ready as I'd ever be for his reaction. The knot in my stomach melted when he smiled.

Darren's solid professional background helped in the analysis of interactions between himself and the young prince during our trip through time. We compared impressions and discussed the possibility of repercussions, then and now. Inconsequential details were set aside. Whether it was Toltec or Aztec, exactly where or when it happened, was of little concern. The undeniable terrors faced and mastered in that jungle and their impact on the rest of that life had changed the world for the better in countless ways. As to how it could have happened, we had no clue.

Darren confided how immensely rewarding the opportunity to spontaneously comfort and guide a seven-year-old through the almost superhuman challenges of a primitive puberty rite had been. His work at the Mental Health Board dealt exclusively with adults. He knew full well his positive input had enabled the child to emerge from the adventure a powerful force for good.

Darren thoughtfully made note of the similarities between the chief-in-training and himself. We agreed the psychological profiles of the two lifetimes were remarkably similar.

"This was a whole lot more than I expected," he commented as we hugged goodbye. "I've got quite a lot to think about here."

Fresh Out of Excuses

What a relief—the almost empty subway car offered a chance to deal with my own issues. The spontaneous regressions had been so dramatic and exciting, there was no time to question anything. Logical analysis from a new perspective might reveal at least some answers.

Okay, that first regression was easy to rationalize as a fluke. The three subsequent regressions were impossible to explain away, except possibly as a result of expectations built up by the first one. This was a new ball game. The cosmic crash course hurtled on at a dizzying pace. Without Spirit as navigator, I would have been terrified. Even so, shuttling between lifetimes was mind-boggling.

The truth was the regressions weren't just happening around me —they were happening through me. This added a new and unsettling dimension to my commitment to serve as an instrument of Divine Purpose. It had taken me half a lifetime to accept my healing abilities. These five transmogrifying events had left me unhinged.

This success was much scarier than failure. How could I possibly embrace a completely different concept of reality in one month? Where to begin? Which version of reality was really real? But that was no project for a subway ride. Logic could wait. At least for now, I could sit back and be grateful for the miracles that were happening.

Home at last, the wheels wouldn't stop turning. Darren's easy transport through time demolished my only theory as to what had generated these phenomena. The incarnation he visited fit his psychological profile perfectly. How he got there defied explanation, but for my own sanity I had to find one.

A successful private session accelerated the pace. Word spread about these adventures into other lifetimes. It became easier to work with clients than to refuse their requests. They were informed it wasn't hypnotic past life regression and it might not work. The non-hypnotic, non-regression sessions did work, but what to call them? Some called them *Soul Voyages*.

Meanwhile, evidence of benefits derived from trips to other lifetimes accumulated. Darren's ongoing response to the jungle experience exceeded reasonable expectations. The psychological training that enabled him to bond with the mini warrior served him even better in his current lifetime. The personal awareness and understanding acquired during the puberty rites led to breakthroughs in self-mastery that could well have taken years in traditional therapy. Though small in stature, he prided himself on his athletic endurance. Friends tried to understand why such a professional therapist would drive himself so mercilessly. The jungle experience lent a different perspective to his idiosyncracies.

Though Darren couldn't foresee making radical changes in his headlong approach to life, he did resolve to be kinder in his self-judgment. Over the next few months he gave himself permission to enjoy life. He spent more quality time with his girlfriend and made more space for fun and relaxation.

Lorna's ongoing fringe benefits, subtle but life enhancing, took a bit of time to manifest. In early classes she avoided sitting on the same side of the room with an older man. She couldn't explain her reaction to men, especially older men. Her husband, who was younger than she, was the only man she'd ever trusted.

A warm friendship with an older gentleman in the group was an enormous personal triumph. She attributed it to a karmic release when the pioneer woman forgave her husband.

Vivian seemed stronger, more confident and energetic. She was convinced Spirit's healing of the noble African had changed her life.

Subtle changes occurred in the group consciousness. It was not surprising, considering the miraculous events that had become our new norm. All we could do was let the consciousness expansion land where it might.

The next few healing classes grew larger and attracted new students, some of whom brought their own expertise. It eventually wound down when Bobbi announced she had joined a dance troupe and wouldn't be available for classes. I suggested the possibility of meeting at my home in Forest Hills. We closed with a tentative agreement to discuss future plans.

Manhattanites' reluctance to travel to Queens all but ended the classes. Isolated from the small group who knew me and my story, I didn't know where to turn. Obstacles loomed large. In the excitement and wonder of the classes, my "ordinary" healing work had been set aside. Also, travel time was a problem. My career seemed to have taken a cosmic U-turn on the way to a healing.

Contact with Spirit was tremendously rewarding, both emotionally and spiritually, but it didn't pay the rent. It was time to integrate my two worlds. It would take a real paradigm shift to fit all the new truths and alternate perspectives into my old version of sanity.

Reluctant Convert

Soul Voyages took concentration and energy, but more than that, openness and discipline I didn't know I had. It was a constant challenge to listen, learn and integrate new truths and alternate parameters into what I used to think was reality. A lifetime of rationalization techniques I'd used to convince myself all those spontaneous healings were "just ordinary massages" no longer worked. It would take more than a little courage to redefine reality, and change core beliefs. Unfortunately, my only support system was a long way away. At least with Spirit's help it shouldn't take 25 years to finally admit what I'm doing.

My dual-hemispheric world was fraught with unexpected complications. Simultaneous awareness of two separate incarnations, plus Spirit, required a strange kind of unfocused concentration. Returning to a so-called normal frame of reference was tricky. Left hemispheric activities like names, logistics and math took quite a toll. In an approximation of normalcy, I smiled my way through, agreed with things I couldn't later recall, and bumped into things a lot.

There were some humorous moments. More than once I made off-the-wall comments that left people looking at me rather strangely. Through it all, a burgeoning sense of rightness and order in the universe shone through the confusion. The intra-incarnational sessions convinced me that what we see, hear and do in other lifetimes is embedded somewhere deep within the consciousness, whether we remember it or not. For want of a better definition, this is permanent healing on the core consciousness level, the only place that matters.

Chapter Four
There and Back Again

Excitement built steadily in New York's close-knit metaphysical community. Everyone assumed it was past life regression, a standard technique offered by trained hypnotists with impressive credentials. With the referrals came questions about how this mysterious new technique worked. It was almost painful explaining that it wasn't past life regression, especially since I was so bereft of credentials.

How could I explain the multiple differences between hypnotic regression and this new technique, when most of the work was done by a high-powered Spirit Guide whose name I didn't even know? Also, there was no guarantee that it would work with "civilians." So far I had only dealt with students.

Things got back to a semblance of normal when a healing client referred a brilliant PhD clinical psychologist for a healing. Meg, a lovely soft blonde in frail health, had sought alternative therapy after years of failed medical treatments. We met in the West Side apartment of a colleague.

The prospect of working with a PhD university professor was daunting, but in no time Meg felt at ease. We began the spiritual healing working with traumatic issues in her present life. She enjoyed the energy and was more than pleased with the results. Progress seemed slow compared to blitz trips through time. From her standpoint it was lightning fast.

Backwards—and How!

Early in the third session, Spirit took charge. Without warning, Meg was transported to a filthy hovel. The lone occupant was a retarded girl. We were both speechless. Thankfully Spirit was not. I heard my voice utter attempts to reach her. At first, we humans suspected she was mute.

Meg was ready to throw in the towel. By the standards and practices of modern psychology, the girl in the hovel was beyond help.

Gently maneuvering past Meg's resistance, Spirit asked, "What is she doing?" The question was so logical, an unfiltered answer slipped past her usual reserve.

"She's so limited! She can hardly do anything at all! There's no use trying to reach her!" Meg gritted out.

Once again came the soft, confident directive, "Observe more carefully. Tell me what she is doing and how she is doing it."

Curiosity piqued, Meg rose to the challenge. "Oh! Well, she's sorting grains." A note of tenderness crept into her voice. "Really, she's doing it quite carefully and nicely, turning the grains over one at a time." With that the girl became a person instead of a creature barely above animal status.

"Speak to her," Spirit prompted. "See if you can reach her."

"What are you doing?" Meg asked.

"Make for to eat," the girl responded. Her voice came out slurred and deep, startling us both. But the therapist had made first contact and was not about to let the moment pass.

"Do you live with anyone?" she asked.

"Hmm mmm," Meg's head shook in denial.

"Do you have any friends?"

"Hmm mmm," more emphatic head shaking.

"Why are you living all alone here?"

"No like."

"You don't like people?"

"Hmm mmm. No like me... say I crazy."

"I see. So you see no one?" Meg asked, her skillful questions deepening the connection..

My mind began to wander. After all, I wasn't needed here. The wisest being I'd ever encountered and a brilliant PhD were running the show. All I had to do was stay plugged in to the cosmic energy field. "Is it possible that this poor creature is totally isolated?" I wondered.

"Just father... er, the priest," the girl mumbled.

"Does he come often?"

"Moon time he come."

"At night?"

"Hmm umm, big moon, little moon, 'nother big moon he come, bring things."

Meg's skills and training had broken through this poor creature's fear. This required understanding beyond an average academic. My respect for Meg was growing by the minute.

"What does the father call you?" Meg probed.

"Liana."

"Do you like living here, all alone, Liana?"

"No like people. Animals much nicer. Trees much nicer. Don't call me names, throw rocks."

The patient questioning seemed torturously slow, but I was spellbound. I had to remind myself to keep the energy flowing and let Spirit use my voice.

With great tenderness, Meg assured Liana that the people who had hurt her were ignorant and cruel. Then with professional authority she announced, "I think I've done all I can do here."

Instead of praise for a job well done, Spirit issued a challenge. "What could you possibly have done in an earlier lifetime that would make you punish yourself so unmercifully?"

Shocked and rebellious, Meg curled into a fetal position and retreated into silence.

"You think you understand it all—the trail of cruelty, conditioned reflex and habitual response of one narrowly constricted lifetime," Spirit calmly asserted. "Do you think that is the end of it? Open your mind. your heart, your spirit, and you will see that those patterns persist… difficult to penetrate but often vastly powerful… from lifetime to lifetime.

"Huh?" my left hemisphere snapped to full attention. Now I was hanging onto every word that came through my mouth. So far these sessions had dealt with one incarnation, a singular situation… one! This was completely different! Spirit had addressed the situation, defined the issue and then challenged Meg to contemplate life-to-life cause and effect. This turned abstract speculations I'd toyed with into a valid working theory. Icy shivers shot through my body.

"You must follow the trail of cause and effect from other lifetimes to be able to understand any single life pattern," Spirit continued.

"How can I… uh, how could that possibly happen?" Meg stammered.

"Use your well-practiced meditative skills. Let go of your stranglehold on a limited, finite version of reality. That which you can see, touch and anticipate is a tiny fragment of the whole. Relax your body… your mind… and ask to be taken to another place, another time, where something happened that made your soul decide to punish itself so dreadfully," our guide intoned.

I held my breath, not knowing what might happen… or not. Meg was accustomed to being the expert in charge. Our work required giving up control.

From Hovel to Palace

To our astonishment, transport happened instantaneously. A startled gasp burst from Meg, then a look of profound wonderment lit her face.

"I'm in a mansion, it looks like… or a palace. Rich dark carved woods, stone walls, heroic bronze statues, tapestries and huge candelabra. There's a woman poised on the staircase."

"Can you describe her?"

"She's a patrician beauty with raven hair, a slim, graceful body and an air of command. She's wearing a full-length crimson satin gown. It flows along the thickly carpeted stairs. This looks like a magnificent Renaissance style mansion."

Any possible connection to Liana eluded me entirely.

Meg could barely register the enormous disparity between the two lifetimes before the lady of the manor issued a riveting, imperious challenge: "Who are you and what are you doing here?" she demanded in a sultry voice totally unrecognizable as Meg.

Spirit answered easily, "My lady… we have come a long way, through space and time, to assist you."

"*You*? Help *me*?" she laughed contemptuously.

"What help could she possibly need?" I wondered. "Looks like this lady already has everything, and a tad more."

"I'm a stranger here. Could you tell me where we are?" I blurted before I could catch myself.

"You're in Italy, in the home of an aristocrat, a great man—my father."

"Won't you be so kind as to tell us your name so we can converse normally?" Spirit continued. "We are here to assist you in any way that might serve you."

"You may call me Caterina," she answered haughtily.

"You are a very beautiful woman," Spirit commented.

"Do Spirits really notice those things?" I wondered. "Is this appreciation of physical beauty or acknowledgement that it is an issue? What an interesting idea."

"I've always been beautiful," she grudgingly responded, "It's a curse!"

"Is that not an advantage in marriage?" the quiet, understated Spirit voice countered.

"I am not married—nor shall I ever be!"

"Why? You are so lovely; there must have been many suitors."

"I am unfit!!" Caterina issued forth like a biblical proclamation.

"Unfit? How can that be?" I wondered. "She's obviously brilliant, talented, beautiful and rich!"

Soul Therapy

Once again Spirit issued a challenge. "You are a skilled therapist. This woman requires your compassion and expertise to conquer her self-hatred and shame. You must help."

I almost lost it. "Where did that come from?" I wondered. "Meg is in a state of near exhaustion. How can she go on? Is it even possible to practice psychotherapy on another incarnation?"

Meg wearily rose to the professional challenge and worked her magic on the aristocratic lady. Wasting no time with platitudes, she dove into the heart of the matter. A few well-placed questions uncovered the source of her self-loathing and guilt. With consummate skill, Meg drew forth the details of an all-too-familiar story.

"I was always my father's favorite," Caterina grudgingly revealed. "We had a close, loving relationship. My mother could never compete with the wonderful stories, the secret gifts, the enchantment he wove.

"I was fast to learn and anxious to please," she sighed, "and my father was my prince charming. He called me his princess, his darling and taught me how to make him happy. He took me to a magical place on my third birthday. My mother wasn't invited. It was our secret and she couldn't know."

"Oh, my dear!" A tear traced Meg's cheek as the lady whispered her terrible secret.

"I'm ashamed… I must have tempted him," Caterina muttered.

Meg fought passionately to overcome the terrible guilt that consumed this lovely woman. "This is not your fault," she cried passionately. "The blame here is his, not yours. You were just a baby. He was the adult! The responsibility was his, not yours!"

"Brava!" I silently applauded, completely swept up in the drama.

Unrelentingly, Meg whittled away at the deeply embedded conviction that she should suffer for her sins. The laborious procedure to help this conscience-stricken victim seemed endless. With masterful 20th Century expertise she peeled away the layers of Caterina's carefully constructed reality.

"How could a three-year-old possibly seduce a sophisticated, worldly adult?" Meg demanded.

"I never thought about that."

"Who instigated what?" Meg persisted.

"What do you mean?"

"Where did this take place?"

"He always took me… oh… I see what you mean."

"Where was your mother?"

"She was busy… doing things for my father. Oh! Oh! Oh!" she stammered, suddenly overcome with full comprehension.

"How could you have resisted?" Meg countered. "How can you take the blame for wanting to please your Daddy and make him happy?"

Dead silence.

Meg had finally broken through the wall of pain and self-loathing this poor woman had interred herself within. Then, with consummate skill, she set about reinforcing the positive aspects of Caterina's innate decency and courage.

At exactly the right moment, Spirit spoke directly to Caterina and gave instructions to move forward within her lifetime.

"Tell us about your life, Caterina, how you lived it once you were on your own. What have you accomplished? What have you done with your life?"

Caterina looked about, startled at the request.

Then in an aside to Meg, Spirit urged, "You know how to draw her out. Help her to recognize her worth."

"So it's up to me?" Meg sighed deeply and stoically pressed on. "Tell me... what you are doing now, Caterina?"

"It is time to retire to my quarters. The audience is over."

"The audience?"

"As successor to my father, it is my duty to run things... to mediate quarrels, assign duties, grant rewards. I do what must be done. I hear their complaints... the serfs, workers, merchants and craftsmen who live in my realm. I resolve disputes, issue orders... hold court... mete out the fairest justice I'm capable of. Enough! I am done with you!"

Spirit was not nearly finished with Caterina, or with the matter at hand. "Do you do things the same way your father did before you... or have you made changes in the system?"

That refueled the dialogue.

"As a woman alone it was necessary to rely upon the hard work and good will of my servants and serfs as well as my suppliers. I found I had a sense of who was trustworthy and whom I needed to hold accountable. Those who abuse their privileges are banished rather than imprisoned. I have no taste for torture, nor room for prisons."

I was stunned. The mature Caterina had really made a difference in her world. She had just described outstanding humanitarian policies unheard of in her time and social milieu. Yet she continued to consider herself worthless. Remarkable!

"This is an admirable accomplishment," Spirit declared. "You have created an enclave of peace and harmony here within your estate. How have you managed all this?" asked our guide.

"It's nothing, really. I simply give credit where it is due. Here we reward hard work with praise and privilege."

"How generous. Common people rarely know such fairness. What must they do to be so rewarded?" Spirit prompted.

"It is not too difficult—just work harder and steal less. The most productive serfs are given full ownership of their land once they have earned it. They work all the harder to win their freedom."

"Her loyal servants must have lived very well indeed according to the standards of the day," I ruminated. "If anyone deserves a heavenly reward, it certainly is she. Yet with irrational perseverance, she insists she is not fit for heaven."

At Spirit's insistence a nearly exhausted Meg gave it her best shot. "You must see it! Surely you cannot deny the good you've done… God knows you are innocent. It is a crime to deny yourself your justly earned reward."

Caterina reluctantly agreed to go to the most perfect place in the cosmos… where she was convinced she didn't belong. Spirit issued instructions to float away from Earth and into the protection of waiting Spirit guides. She left with a whoosh.

Back to a New Future

After that splendid psychoanalytic *tour de force* Meg, thoroughly spent, sighed with relief. We both assumed that it was a job well done.

Spirit, not yet satisfied, calmly announced, "Now it's time to visit Liana once more."

"Go back to that hovel in the woods? Not quite!" Meg shuddered.

Spirit was insistent, so back we went… but where?

Assuming she'd landed in the wrong place, Meg mumbled, "I must have gotten lost. This can't be the same girl… the same place."

Spirit urged her to describe what she saw.

"She's at a stream, actually washing her clothes!" Meg cried.

"She's where?" my shocked left hemisphere demanded. "What stream? Did I miss something?"

In sheer astonishment Meg choked, "Everything's changed. She seems to be moving into a more normal life. Why, there are people around her now. Oh! A little child is coming over to her. She's asking what was the matter with her before. Liana is so embarrassed. She doesn't know what to say." Her body was tense with empathy.

"Tell her to say she used to be sick but now she's better," Spirit suggested.

That was exactly the right thing to say. Meg's shoulders dropped a couple of notches as she gently assured Liana.

"She's whispering in the child's ear," Meg reported. "The child is nodding and smiling. I do think Liana's going to be all right. But how could this happen?" she gasped.

Thrilled with the outcome, but totally confused, I echoed that question. Had the fruit of Meg's labor, the almost magical restoration of Caterina's self-worth, somehow changed Liana's karma? It seemed impossible.

Spirit succinctly encapsulated a karmic revelation. "All beliefs and assumptions about reincarnation are invalid, imperfect… wrong," and was gone. That revelation sent me into a state of transcendent wonder.

Meg was back, thoroughly depleted, but profoundly moved. The juggernaut effect was overwhelming. We were both disoriented, with an awful lot of digesting to do.

"There's no doubt," Meg mumbled distractedly, "that certain physical conditions I've been suffering from that have defied conventional medicine can be linked to that second lifetime and Caterina. Later… now sleep… preferably about twelve hours of sleep!"

What Have We Wrought?

On the way back to Queens, my thoughts went ballistic. It was as if Meg and I had unwittingly entered the Twilight Zone. To downplay or dismiss the experience as fantasy was unthinkable. Every detail was as clear, powerful and undeniably real as our daily lives. Conflicted and confused, I somehow made it home and collapsed.

Morning was laden with questions. Where was it written that one could relive events from two "past lives," resolve emotional issues, follow through with positive actions, and thereby change those lives? And what might the changes we make in past lives do to our current lives?

In long telephone conversations over the next few weeks, Meg and I diligently dissected and analyzed those two altered lives. We knew it was a great privilege to witness the spiritual evolution of two people whose gravestones have almost certainly crumbled away by now. The two separate but unequal versions of Caterina and Liana's lives were unprecedented as far as we knew. According to the Law of Cause and

Effect (karma?), good or bad actions have consequences in subsequent lives.

"What's done is done" seemed obsolescent compared to the revisionist history we'd just lived through. Was this the new reality? What infinite possibilities awaited us in the transcendental realm now unfolding!

Over the next few weeks Meg experienced a miraculous recovery from a medical condition that had plagued her for years. Implausible as it might seem, we could only attribute it to reversal of causative factors. When Spirit and Caterina rewrote history it eliminated her karmic trail of guilt.

We laughed about "New Age" people who used karma stories as a convenient excuse to avoid opportunities to grow. The catchall phrase, "My karma made me do it," rang more hollow than ever before.

In retrospect, we had to agree that her session had shattered the traditional concept that the bondage of karma can only be overcome through the humiliation, suffering, and great effort of many lifetimes. Liana's instant karmic healing was a far cry from endless incarnations of suffering in retribution for past sins. Diligent research failed to unearth published records of karma literally erased by altering the "past." Neither of us had been able to discover any record that karma and punishment from one life could be erased through the enlightenment of a prior incarnation. Had such instant karmic resolution ever occurred? Who could say? Finally, we decided to just give thanks for the miracle and say goodnight.

Chapter Five
At the Feet of the Master

A sorting-out of all these mysteries was way overdue. Since I couldn't discuss them with most people, I really needed a sounding board. It might relieve the tension to have a third-party opinion. On impulse I called my friend Teri, a yoga instructor with a guru. Over a cup of tea, I hesitantly asked if she had ever heard of traveling into other lifetimes.

Her reaction didn't exactly relieve my anxiety. Suddenly she blurted, "Are you talking about reincarnation? And what do you mean by traveling to other lifetimes?" I proceeded to give her a Readers' Digest version of the startling events occurring in my life. Teri was enthralled with the narrative. She demanded more and more details about the events I'd hinted at. In no time she'd wrested a full confession from me.

The doubting questions I'd expected never came. Instead she exploded with excitement and requested a session of her own. Those inexplicable encounters with other lifetimes ignited a chord of unfulfilled longing.

"I must do this as soon as possible," she exclaimed.

"You're welcome to attend our classes," I countered.

"Oh, no, I couldn't possibly do this in public!" she insisted. Then she confided, "I have been told that once I sat at the feet of the Master and that I will accept no human teacher until we met again." Her request was as urgent as it was unexpected.

Logic Please!

There went the unbiased feedback I'd hoped for! Teri could not be relied upon for objectivity. Things were going from bad to worse.

Teri simply couldn't wait. I finally agreed to see her privately. She picked up the phone and to my amazement, proceeded to talk her boyfriend into a dual session.

How could this be happening? Bud, a former WWII pilot, was a pragmatic intellectual. Would he call it mumbo jumbo? Sleep didn't come easily that night.

The next evening Teri, with a somewhat reluctant Bud in tow, arrived for her avidly anticipated session. Given the choice, he was more than willing for her to go first.

Teri approached her journey with quiet confidence. Adept at yoga meditation, she quickly slipped into an altered state of consciousness. She floated through time, easily following the now familiar instructions to go to another lifetime in which something important to here and now was happening. She was catapulted into the last place she could have imagined.

Right Religion—Wrong Destination

To her utter dismay, my Jewish friend landed a long way from Jerusalem. Stunned nearly speechless, she described the person to whom she was drawn.

"It's a nun… very young and sweet. She's on her knees, dressed in a traditional nun's habit… that long black thing! And she's scrubbing flagstones in a courtyard."

Out of the corner of my eye I caught sight of Bud, his eyes rolling in disbelief.

The eager young nun seemed quite content with her lot. Teri was definitely not.

"How often do you scrub this pathway?" I asked.

"This is my job," the nun responded sweetly, "I do it every day."

"Doesn't anyone else take turns doing this job?"

"Oh, no, Mother Superior says it's good for my soul…"

I got a flash of a thin, ferociously uncompromising tyrant and shivered. Teri's body tensed in irritation. Correction, make that cold fury.

"How could anyone possibly tolerate this drudgery, this abuse?" she demanded.

Bye Bye Bad Karma

My heart was with her. "This is a mighty long way from kneeling at the feet of the Master," I mused. "How can I help her through this?" Then Spirit arrived and my mouth was saying something entirely different from what was going on in my head.

"Let's go forward in time a bit… I'll count you through," came the gentle prompting. "One… two… three. Now tell me where you are and what's happening."

There she was, the same little nun… much older and badly worn, but still scrubbing away at those very same flagstones.

"She must be in terrible pain," Teri moaned. "Her knees are nothing but open sores."

The forecast was endless repetitive hardship, obligatory religious observance and nonstop flagstone scrubbing. Totally disillusioned with this version of the religious life Teri again broke through, interrupting the pious nun's meek platitudes mid-sentence.

"I'm stuck! I'm stuck!" she cried out furiously. "This is not spiritual! This is not spiritual at all! There's no way to serve the world… no way to make a contribution. This is slavery! I want out of here!"

"Who could blame her?" I thought. It was uncomfortable just listening to the platitudes that justified a life of physical agony and thankless servitude.

Our Spirit mentor neatly took the cue. "Let's go to another place, another time, where another aspect of your Whole Self is experiencing events that influence your current life."

Gulp! "There Spirit goes with another new concept—the 'Whole Self.' Hmm." I tucked it away for future analysis.

We leapt effortlessly into another lifetime in pursuit of a more elevating experience. The next encounter was more surprising than the last.

At Spirit's urging, Teri glibly described her surroundings. "It's a bright, sunny day in 16th century Italy."

Gone was the meek, homily-burdened murmur. The energy was definitely male… a rather dominant male.

"Please tell me about yourself," Spirit encouraged.

"I'm a merchant, middle aged I suppose you'd say. My name is Guillermo. I'm wearing very fine clothes."

"Can you please tell us where you are?"

Mary Blake

Risk and Ruination

"I'm at a seaport in the south. I can't stop pacing… back and forth… back and forth. Something's not right."

"What is wrong, Guillermo?" we asked.

"My ship is overdue! I'm worried. It should have arrived by now," he blurted.

"Perhaps it's delayed by weather?"

"No, no, no! Other ships have been arriving every day. Mine is the only one behind schedule. Everything I own is tied up in that cargo. I was counting on it to make my fortune," came his grim reply. "I'm afraid something has gone terribly wrong."

"You took a chance and staked your entire fortune on this one cargo?" Spirit gently prompted. "Is that why you're so distraught?"

"Yes! If anything happens to that ship I'm ruined!" jerked out of him.

Spirit moved us forward in time day by day. Guillermo's frustration and sense of impending doom grew as days passed with no word. Then a ship captain reported, "Your ship was attacked and captured by pirates. My own vessel was near enough to witness the crime by spyglass, but we were too far away to attempt a rescue."

"I'm destitute!" Guillermo cried. "Everything I've worked for my whole life is gone. I'm done for!"

"What are your options?" our surprisingly pragmatic Spirit guide inquired.

Silence… Guillermo was devastated.

"Is there anyone you can borrow from?" Spirit persisted.

"It's hopeless. I've exhausted all the usual sources. I even borrowed against future profits. I'm not just broke; I'm indebted to everyone who might have been willing to lend me money. Without that ship, without its cargo, I cannot possibly earn enough to pay my debts… ever!"

My empathy was going full blast. I knew full well what this meant. He faced crushing debt, obligations he could never fulfill, loss of status, shame and disgrace.

Succumbing to self-pity, he bemoaned his fate, "How can I continue? How can I face my wife and children? They know nothing of my desperate gamble. How can I explain? What can I do?"

"Poor guy," I thought, "he's really made a mess of things."

"Your wife and children must be housed, clothed and fed," Spirit countered. "If your usual way of doing that is gone, you must find another way to survive until you can rebuild your fortune. What about relatives?"

"I have no family… they're all dead."

"There's your wife's family, I believe…"

"Accept charity from my in-laws?" he sneered. "That's a prospect worse than death."

"Worse than your children going hungry, living on the street; worse than your wife becoming a servant; worse than debtor's prison?" an uncompromisingly blunt Spirit shot back.

"No, no, no…. never!" he gasped.

"Then you must swallow your pride and tell them your plight. They will help."

"My wife comes from the far North. Her family is very wealthy. That's why I gambled everything on this voyage… to give her what she was always accustomed to. But you are right. I must do what I must."

"Can this guy deal with the humiliation?" I wondered. Asking for money from his in-laws would cut deep into his masculine pride.

Stuck!

Teri wasn't nearly as understanding. Beyond exasperation, she shouted, "I'm stuck! Again, I'm stuck! Get me out of here! I've had it! I want to come back!"

Back we came.

Teri sat up, dejected and thoroughly disillusioned. "That's it, then," she sighed mournfully, "I really didn't study at the feet of the Master. They lied to me!"

Feeling her pain, I tried my best to comfort and reassure my friend. "Just because you weren't taken to a lifetime with 'the Master' isn't absolute proof that you were never there. Perhaps you were with the Master in a lifetime we didn't visit," I suggested. "Maybe the two lifetimes you were taken to provided important information that will be valuable to you here and now. Remember, the instructions were to go to a place where something important to your current lifetime was happening. The hardships of those two lifetimes might explain a great deal about this one. Meditate on them. It will probably become a lot clearer as you think it through. Give yourself time. Don't be so quick to pass judgment."

Privately, I suspected it might have something to do with pride. I kept that thought to myself because it wouldn't be helpful, especially since she was too vulnerable to hear it now. She'd probably work it through on her own.

"Well," she sighed, "I guess it's Bud's turn… that is if he hasn't changed his mind."

Bud had succumbed to boredom and was gently snoring away. Stung by what she considered a fiasco, Teri sat tensely, anticipating sardonic comments about a wasted evening when he awoke.

Contrary to all expectations, Bud agreed to "take a stab at it." This highly intelligent loner excelled at investments, analysis and technical, physical, very masculine activities. He claimed to be allergic to religion and quickly extracted himself from any conversation that seemed to be heading toward the spiritual. A parochial school in Chicago had spawned a lifelong aversion to religion.

As for Teri's yoga studies and meditation, he'd quip lightly, "She does her thing and I do mine. I don't make her fly airplanes and she doesn't make me go to ashrams."

One could hardly blame us for harboring doubts.

Chapter Six
Of Camels, Wives and Other Treasures

Our first task was to somehow accommodate Bud's oversized frame. He was longer than my couch. Teri and I managed to cantilever a cushion on the arm of the couch for his feet and there he lay, all six foot five inches neatly balanced.

Assuming Bud had never been exposed to meditation, I improvised some manly relaxation and deep breathing techniques to enable him to go into the requisite state of altered consciousness. The concentration skills that served Bud so well as a WWII fighter pilot enabled him to quickly segue into a scene right out of Lawrence of Arabia. The first port of call was as revealing of the man on my couch as of the character in the desert. Silently I prayed Spirit was still with us and was soon relieved.

"What may we call you, sir?" Spirit asked.

"My name is Akmed."

"Can you describe yourself, please?"

"I am a caravan driver, what else?" came the casual response.

I suspected he was a bit more than a driver. His affect was that of a powerful caravan owner, a buccaneer plowing the seas of sand in pursuit of spoils and adventure.

"Where do you go with your caravan? What route do you take?"

"All the way to the end… the Orient."

"Like Marco Polo?" Spirit queried. "It must be an interesting life."

A terse nod acknowledged the obvious.

"What do you purchase along your route?" our remarkably practical Spirit inquired.

Akmed spoke with the self-assurance of a well-seasoned, successful entrepreneur. "I purchase ornate goods from India and the Orient… decorative brass trays, jewelry, precious stones, carvings."

"And what do you bring with you to exchange?"

"Primitive things… raw materials… sheepskins, wool, stone, wood and other basic materials that are much in demand at the other end of the caravan route."

"You must do quite well," Spirit commented.

Reluctantly, with the attitude of one attempting to reveal as little as possible, he admitted to being "more than a little comfortable."

That reluctance was a clincher. It rang true for me.

"It shows," came the quietly confident response from our spiritual friend.

"Well, yes…" he chuckled.

"A person of your stature must have camels…"

"Many," came the laconic response.

"Do you have horses?"

"About twenty-five. I believe you call them 'Arabian,'" was his amused comment.

"Are you married?"

With an air of distracted boredom he responded, "Of course. I have six wives."

Teri and I were fascinated, hungry for more details.

Bud's somewhat weary voice interrupted, "I think we've discovered all there is to know here. Let's go somewhere else."

Spirit obligingly provided ways and means to do just that. Bud confidently followed instructions.

Bye Bye Bad Karma

Simon

"Somewhere else" turned out to be nothing short of heart-stopping.

After a brief whirl in the void Bud's posture, even his features, altered completely. A somber, sorrowful expression overlaid his usual self-assured countenance.

"Can you describe your surroundings?" Spirit inquired gently.

The answer came in muted tones of despair. "I'm standing on a hill watching the crucifixion."

"What crucifixion?"

"*The* crucifixion!"

I could scarcely breathe. A muffled gasp told me Teri was as shocked as I.

Spirit calmly asked, "How are you feeling?"

"I'm shattered!" he gasped.

"How are you dressed?"

"In tatters."

"What is your name?"

"Simon."

"Hmm," I ventured, unable to hold back, "I've heard that name. I believe one of the Apostles…"

"Yes," he interrupted, "but I'm not one of 'The Twelve.' I'm just a follower, an ordinary person."

He went on, sorrowfully describing the agony and despair of the scene. "His mother is crying. Everyone is crying. Even some of the Roman soldiers are crying. We're all devastated."

Spirit deftly inched us forward a day or two. "What is happening now?"

"Same as yesterday," he mumbled. "Now they're dragging his body down from the cross."

I was stunned at the personal insights and opinions woven in his first-hand account of this world changing event. Teri was mesmerized.

Simon lapsed into silence.

At The Grove

"Now what's happening?" Spirit encouraged.

"I'm following along with the other mourners on the way to the grove." His voice registered indescribably deep sadness. "You know," he opined thoughtfully, "as I think about it, this was inevitable. He was just getting to be too popular. That's not healthy. Those in power don't like that much at all."

Spirit instructed him to go forward to the next important event. "What's happening now, Simon?" he prompted.

"A few days have passed and I'm back at the burial cave."

During a long silence punctuated by sharp intakes of breath, Simon struggled to get his emotions under control.

"What are you doing?" Spirit inquired.

"I'm examining the side of the cave. I can't figure this out. There are no marks on it! How could this be? It would take at least six men to move that stone!"

In response to Spirit's prompts, Simon described events as they unfolded.

"I've heard rumors about the Master," Spirit inquired casually. "What do you think?"

"Yeah, I've heard those rumors too," Simon responded in a voice betraying healthy skepticism. "You couldn't prove it by me. I haven't seen Him. I'm not going to believe it unless I see it."

I couldn't help thinking how much this Simon reminded me of our Bud.

Conversion of a Skeptic

Spirit moved us forward in time yet another day and gently asked what was happening. Utterly transformed, Simon blurted, "I've seen Him, the Master. At first I didn't recognize Him. We were just walking along… and then He spoke to me. I couldn't believe it was Him." His voice trembled with reverence.

"Then what happened?" I blurted, losing the battle to keep silent.

"He showed me his wounds to prove who He was. That was enough!

Bye Bye Bad Karma

I didn't have to touch them."

"What did 'the Master' say?" Spirit inquired.

"He told me to go out and spread the word, to teach others the things he had taught us."

"What are you going to do now?"

He barked a short laugh, "I'm going to go out and teach!"

"Where are you going to teach?"

"I thought I'd start out in Damascus, the city where I was born."

"Do you have a special place in mind?"

"I plan to start right near the great temple."

"Why would you choose to locate there?"

"Well logically, if you want to teach, you go where the most people are. The great temple is the center of town."

Leaping forward about a year, Spirit again addressed Simon of Damascus. "How are you? How's the teaching going?"

"Well, it's going rather well," he responded. "I have quite a few followers here but I'm getting a bit nervous. You have to get a little uneasy when the numbers start adding up. It's different when there's just a few followers. That's what happened with the Master, you know. His popularity was what caused them to make their move. The 'Powers that Be' don't like it when the crowds start gathering."

"I see," said Spirit. "Let's go forward in time three more years."

A strange stillness descended upon the room.

Unable to bear the suspense, I blurted, "Where is Simon of Damascus?"

"Dead," came the quiet, matter-of-fact response. Suddenly a profoundly moved Bud was back with us. There was no trace of the slightly amused, worldly skeptic tolerantly humoring his naïve girlfriend.

"Well, that was quite an experience," Bud mused. "It was the last thing in the world I would have expected. I thought I was permanently cured of religion by the nuns in Catholic school. Guess this is one experiment I'll never forget!"

Teri was dejectedly dealing with the disappointment because her chance to prove her connection with "the Master" hadn't materialized. To make things worse, Bud, the nonbeliever, received the profound revelations she longed for. How ironic!

Just short of paralysis, Teri hugged me and put on her coat. They slipped out into the night hand in hand, two thoroughly bewildered people.

Deeply moved, I relived this evening of wonderment. It was one of the most haunting experiences I have ever known. It's impossible to witness such a deeply moving experience without being irrevocably changed.

Afterthoughts

During the following weeks Teri was uncharacteristically but understandably reticent about her personal fiasco. Complete re-ordering of assumptions takes a while, but she was up to the task. In phone conversations, she occasionally spoke wistfully about the unfairness of it all. Why should Bud, who was completely disinterested in spirituality, have had the sacred journey she'd been denied?

Time went by and occasionally we'd get together for jazz concerts. Bud, when asked about hidden spiritual proclivities, would gracefully sidestep. "How about that MJQ?" he'd grin and that was the end of it.

I simply couldn't get that mind-blowing, soul-shattering experience out of my head. It was wondrous how Spirit guided us through those heart-wrenching events without commentary. We were left to draw our own conclusions. Perhaps that's exactly what we needed. It changed all our lives. Bud seemed a lot more relaxed and laid back. Teri lost a bit of her spiritual arrogance. My faith and confidence in the work was deepened. On reflection, I realized there was nothing frivolous or flattering about any of our voyages. This was serious business. However, I was not nearly aware of, or ready to accept, its immense power and potential.

Chapter Seven
Dodging the Medicine Man

Meg called to tell me her brother had decided to make an appointment for a session.

"You're pulling my leg!" I laughed.

"No, he's serious," Meg insisted.

He had casually escorted us to a private space where we could work, then immersed himself in the book he and his roommate were co-authoring.

Art was an intellectual workaholic at the top of his game. I was flattered that such an eminent PhD would be interested in working with a nontraditional therapist like me. "Perhaps something unusual is troubling him," I mused.

I was filled with trepidation and concern that Art might be too busy analyzing and intellectualizing to enter a state of altered consciousness. I needn't have worried. That was the only easy part of the session.

Within seconds of arriving at his destination, Art groaned. Wherever he was, whoever he'd contacted was in agony. Such severe discomfort had to be dealt with immediately.

"He must be furious that he agreed to this session," my conscious mind fretted. I was out of my depth before we even got started. Once again, I sent out a frantic plea, "Spirit, how can we stop this pain?"

Lost

Our unflappable Spirit guide whisked Art backwards through time to discover the origin of his discomfort. Nothing but panting ensued. Moments crept by… far too slowly for me. Just as I was about to throw in the towel, Art's face changed. Layer upon layer of sophistication peeled away.

"Lost!" he sobbed in a very tiny voice. "It's all gone!"

"What's gone?" Spirit probed gently.

"Everything! Everything we knew."

"Everything who knew?" Spirit asked.

"Our family! Our city… our world!"

"You're alive and everything else is gone? How can that be?"

"Someone came… I was supposed to be asleep."

"But you were listening?"

"It was dark and they were whispering, but I heard them. He said 'total'… and then he said, 'Run!'"

"Just like that?"

"The man said we had to get away fast before… before *the end*."

"Why did he say that? Who told him?" Spirit prompted.

"The Keepers of the Secrets," he whispered.

"Why did they want you to run away?"

"To save us… our 'hair-tage.' They said to take only enough to keep us alive. Everything else would be in the boat."

"What happened then?"

"He ran out. My parents came and got me and then we ran away. We ran as fast as we could and still we almost didn't make it. I couldn't run that fast so my mother and father carried me between them to the boat."

"What were you running from?"

"From the 'Nye-hill-ation.'"

"Annihilation?" Spirit amended. "What caused it?"

"I don't know. It was dark and I was sleepy. When I woke up there were big, big waves and the whole sky was on fire. We were afraid the boat would turn over and we would drown, but it didn't."

"What caused the sky to be on fire and the big waves?"

"My father said they were right… that Atlantis was no more.

My mother cried."

"Where are you now?"

"I'm hiding in the jungle and I'm so scared."

"Where are your mother and father?"

"The people with no clothes on killed them." he answered in a numb voice.

"But they didn't kill you?"

"My mother hid me under some leaves and stuff. They didn't see me."

"How long did you stay hidden under the leaves?" Spirit asked.

"I don't know. I slept a lot because we couldn't sleep in the boat. My mother told me not to move."

Blond God

"Let's go forward to the next important thing that happens to you," Spirit suggested.

"The leaves blew away. They found me and now they're dancing all around. I guess they think I'm a God or something. Maybe it's my yellow hair… and the things I know."

"I see. How old are you?"

"I'm about three and a half, I think. But I had already been studying in the school for future leaders and scientists before we left. My father was a scientist and my mother was an artist."

"Are you being well treated?"

"As well as they know how, but it's awful… and everything's filthy… and it's hot… so hot!"

"Let's move forward in time till you're more grown up," Spirit suggested.

Silence… then a grunt.

"How are you feeling?" asked Spirit.

"Hopeless… sticky and filthy and hopeless. I can't do much here that makes any sense. I have to pretend to go along with some of their mumbo jumbo or they won't let me do what little I can do."

"You can be proud of what you have accomplished, whether you realize it or not." Spirit assured him.

"That witch doctor, or medicine man, or whatever he is, fights me every step of the way. He's very jealous. Before I came along he was their god."

"Let's move ahead as you grow and learn about the tribe," Spirit recommended. "Tell me where you are now."

"I'm still in this awful jungle. Now I know no one will ever come to rescue me. I'm already bigger than most of these savages. I think I must be fourteen or so… but there's no way to measure time here."

"Of course. How are you getting along? What is your life like?"

"I have taught them as much as I can. But it's really very little. I was so young when we left…"

Bye Bye Bad Karma

"They listen to you?"

"Oh yes. They worship me. I can't have a moment's peace… and I have to learn all their jungle secrets. I watch everything they do carefully and pretend I already know it all."

"I understand. I'm sure you have helped them as much as you could. Their lives must have been changed by what you've been able to give them."

"But not enough! My knowledge is almost as limited as their willingness to change. The witch doctor still stubbornly fights everything I do. Ahhh, and the heat is unbearable."

"Let's go forward to the next important thing that happens to you."

"I'm lying in this hut. I think I'm dying. I have a terrible fever. They've plastered me with these foul-smelling leaves," he groaned. "It's so hot! I must be feverish. I can't bear this heat!"

"How can we help?" I asked.

"Make that goddamned witch doctor stop shaking that goddamned rattle! It's maddening! I can't stand it! Day and night all he does is shake that rattle and yowl. My head… oh, my head… my head! Please let me die!" he choked.

Spirit mercifully granted his wish. "Float out of your body, higher and higher to the cool air above the jungle. The memory of the pain and heat will fade away."

I have never seen anyone so grateful to leave the Earth plane as Art's long-suffering soul brother.

"Keep going until you reach the edge of Earth's atmosphere," Spirit instructed. "You are now in a space between lifetimes."

Art breathed freely for the first time in the session and as the clarity and wisdom of the Universe seeped into his consciousness, he became peaceful and relaxed.

Cosmic Reassessment

"From where you are now, you can look forward and backward in time. Can you tell us what it was like before you got to that jungle?"

In my little bubble, I was teeming with questions about the potential of looking forward and backwards through time. "Stop! Don't interrupt the flow," I ordered my errant left hemisphere.

"We were citizens of an advanced civilization—Atlantis perhaps. The force of the explosion and the ground swells in the ocean threw our boat off course. We landed on the nearest island, probably Guyana."

"Guyana?"

"I believe that's what you call it."

"That's a very dangerous place, even in the 20th century," I interjected.

"My parents were intellectuals, not fighters. They didn't have a chance."

"And a three-year-old child… why did they keep you alive?" Spirit queried.

"The blond hair. The savages had never seen anyone with blond hair, much less white skin. Their superstition saved me from the fate my father and mother met, but condemned me to a wasted life."

"As you will soon learn," Spirit assured him, "there's no such thing as a wasted life. But before you go on to the spiritual realm, you have an important contribution to make. What advice would you like to give Art?"

"Ah! He already understands much more now. He realizes why he has had such an insatiable appetite for learning. That which was denied me has driven him through many, many lifetimes. He needed this impetus in order to move forward, to get on with his work. He must stop the endless nit picking and finish that book. It will bring enlightenment and much-needed understanding of the human family to many, many people throughout the world."

"Thank you, and now your spirit guides are here, ready to escort you to the spirit world," Spirit assured our blond god, who wasted no time in idle chit-chat. He was already on his way home.

"…and Art, you must take better care of yourself," Spirit insisted. "There is much to be done and no time to waste. Do not delay. Make each moment count." Between-lives counseling concluded, Spirit simply vanished.

For his part, Art was definitely weary of the whole process. "I'm finished here. May I please come back?" Art's normal voice pled.

"It's important to take time to recover from this ordeal," I assured him.

"All I need is a cold shower and to never, ever hear another rattle as long as I live!" he declared vehemently. "I'm coming back…" and back he came.

Neither of us felt like celebrating. We simply sat and stared at each other for a long moment. Something prompted me to insist on seeing him for a straight healing… soon.

With unaccustomed forbearance, Art sighed, "It might be a good idea."

With that small concession, we set the appointment. Art showed me out and headed for the shower. An inexplicable sense of foreboding overrode my usual sense of closure.

Spiritual Jet Lag

Somewhere between realities, I tried to shake the feeling of having forgotten something. Halfway down the subway stairs, disoriented and annoyed at that fragmentary presentiment, I retraced my steps. Central Park at dusk is ideal for park bench meditation, but it didn't help. I had forgotten something, but what?

I sat idly tracking the progress of a red dragon kite. The memory finally surfaced. "It's March! I'm supposed to be at Alex's birthday party." Whew! That was what I forgot!

Mystery solved, a brisk 15-block stroll down Central Park West and the purchase of a birthday card helped me decompress.

I hardly noticed the odd look my mentor gave me as we exchanged hugs. Savoring a sip of wine, I congratulated myself on accidentally arriving where I was supposed to be, and even on time.

"Boy, are you spaced out!" said the face just above my right shoulder.

I snapped back to the cocktail party. "Uh… well… I just got back from Atlantis and I'm still in jet lag," my mouth blurted.

Eyebrows hovering near his hairline forced my critical factors back to near normal. Apparently my recently amended version of reality was "far out" even at our metaphysical teacher's birthday party.

"Get a grip!" my inner voice snapped. A wink, a grin and a nudge brought the eyebrows back to rest.

The buffet table beckoned and I ambled over to its safe refuge. Food is very grounding. There'd be plenty of time to digest the day's events later. Now we celebrate.

Dark Feelings

On the hour-long trip back to Forest Hills I couldn't shake the feeling of imminent disaster.

Meg called over the weekend with a million questions.

"Did Art say it was okay?" I inquired.

"Of course! He told me the whole thing… including the rattle," she responded. "You know I'd respect his privacy if he hadn't confided in me."

"Obviously, but I had to check. Well, right from the beginning it was incredibly real and intense… and totally unexpected. Who could have imagined Art landing in the jungle after a desperate flight from the destruction of Atlantis? I guess he told you all about the heat and the witch doctor."

"That he did! But what was your impression of the session?"

"It resolved some deep-seated self-doubt and cleared the way for brilliant achievement. Spirit gave a powerful endorsement of his book and also strongly urged him to take better care of himself."

"That's good to hear. Anything else?"

"It wasn't like any other session; no happy ending with clarity and resolution. Meg, there's a heavy, dark feeling I can't shake. I'm concerned about his health. I hope he takes Spirit's advice."

"He has been pushing himself," Meg offered. "But you know this book is his main priority. He and Joseph have been working on it for years and it should be ready for publication soon. It's going to be a classic! What a brilliant mind!"

"I know! But please do what you can to encourage him to get a bit more rest, cut down on the cigarettes and drink a few less martinis," I urged.

"I can't promise much. You know Art. He's a double Leo!"

That half-humorous, half serious banter left us with nothing more to say.

Art submitted to only one healing.

As hard as I tried, the healing energy just wasn't enough to overcome whatever was wrong. I worked until the end of his patience and begged him to slow down on the cigarettes and martinis and get a bit of sun and exercise for a change. He seemed disturbed at my concern.

"It's not fair," he complained to Meg. "She told Joseph that his condition would be just fine, but me—she was worried about! Said my condition was serious."

My services were dispensed with.

Chapter Eight
New Digs, New Focus

As the practice grew, commuting from Forest Hills to "the city" became more difficult. There was no way I could coax Manhattanites to trek out to "the boonies." The mountain was not going to come to Booth Street in Forest Hills. Soon it made more sense to move into Manhattan than to juggle logistics between appointments and still be fresh and ready to travel through time with Spirit.

In a temporary sublet on the Upper West Side, the healing classes morphed into a spiritual development course. Though the apartment was less spacious and beautiful, life was easier. People who would never dream of making the trip to Queens began arriving at my new digs.

Jen, a tall, angular, career woman who had recently joined the class, would never have made that commute. Her public relations job left her frazzled and short of time. No way would she have endured that hour-long subway ride.

Over the next few weeks, Jen got in the habit of lingering a few minutes after class. Her innate curiosity was piqued by allusions to spectacular trips into other lifetimes. In that friendly atmosphere of trust she eventually relaxed enough to request a private session.

We arranged for a convenient time. By now I was much more confident about the work. My only reservation was whether Jen could manage to relax enough to have a successful experience.

Jen arrived precisely on time—as usual. As we went over the basic orientation to prepare for the journey, I commented that I might have to take an important phone call during the session. My daughter was in a minor crisis in California and needed some help.

"What will happen if that's the case?" Jen asked.

"I'm sure we can think of something. Spirit is very resourceful, I've noticed."

"Oh, fine. I'll leave it in their capable hands," she grinned.

Life and Hardships and Stew

I needn't have worried. With many channeling classes under her belt, Jen wasted no time dawdling in the astral. She landed neatly next to a busy housewife. I introduced myself and asked her name.

"It's Martha. Martha Scott," came a gentle, feminine response.

"I've come from very far away. Could you tell me where I am?"

"Why, you're in my kitchen."

"What do you like most about your kitchen?" I asked.

"Oh, the fireplace! It's the best part of the house. It keeps us warm and cozy, and it's so big I can cook anything I want to." The shy, humble voice sounded strange issuing from her lips.

"Jen… cooking… no way," I thought.

"Can you tell me what year it is?" I ventured. It seemed a safe enough question. "I'm from another time, and I'm a bit confused."

"Why, it's 1732," the soft, gentle voice so different from the crisp tones of an urban professional affirmed.

"What country is this?"

"We call it Massachusetts," she answered hesitantly.

"And could I ask the name of your town?"

"The closest town is Lynne, but our farm is way out in the country. We're not really in the town," she explained.

The telephone bell startled us both. "Here comes the test," I thought and prayed it wouldn't break the connection. I told Martha I had an errand to do, apologized and asked if it would be okay to come back a little later. Relieved at her gracious reply, I hurried into the other room, did my best to help my daughter, promised to

call back later and slipped back to Jen. She seemed to be sleeping peacefully. Hesitantly I tried to reconnect. "Martha, this is Mary. I'm back. Do you still have time to visit with me?"

Culture Shock

"Of course, but what was that bell?" Martha's voice was full of curiosity.

Torn between relief that she was still with me, and doubts about how to explain the sound, I blurted, "That was my telephone."

"What's a telephone?"

"Uh…. where I come from things are very different from your world," I hesitated, searching for a way to explain something beyond her comprehension. "We live in the same country, but everything has changed. Many things we take for granted might seem very strange to you. The telephone is an invention we use to talk with each other without having to go to their home or place of business."

"Without even a by-your-leave?" her voice registered pure disgust. "We have no need of telephones. We visit!" Then with a little chuckle she threw me a real zinger. "Jen hates telephones. She has to use them, but she hates them."

What a jolt! "How could this woman from the colonies who had never heard of a telephone know how Jen felt about them?" I wondered. "Is she so connected to Jen that she's aware of some of her little quirks?" It felt like things were getting out of hand, so I cancelled the thought.

"Tell me more about your world," Martha inquired sweetly.

After her reaction to the telephone, I measured my words more carefully. "Well, we have big stores where people go to buy things," I ventured, praying for guidance.

"Oh, you mean like the smithy!" she smiled.

"Actually, they're quite different. Some of our stores are larger than your biggest buildings. They sell many different kinds of things, made by many different people, all in one place."

Martha was horrified. "You mean they sell them and they make them not? How do they know they are well and properly made? I would not want to buy from a stranger!"

I was completely flummoxed. What can one say in the face of such logic? Spirit arrived and graciously took charge… bailing me out of the corner I'd boxed myself into. "Thank you so much for welcoming us strangers into your home. You seem to have made a very nice life here. But you haven't said much about your children," Spirit ventured.

I retreated into my little observation post, grateful to be able to observe instead of struggling to strike the right tone and not put my foot in it.

Like it Was

"Two of them died very young. Life is hard on the little ones," she sighed. "My daughter married and my son went off on his own." The layers of sadness in her tone touched my heart.

"That must have been troublesome," Spirit responded. "You and your husband could have used his help, I'm sure."

"He was of his own mind. They quarreled and off he went."

"Do you see or hear from him often?"

"Nary a word since the day he walked away. I packed him up some meat and bread so's to give him a fair start but that was the last of it."

"Your life hasn't been easy."

She pushed a wisp of hair from her forehead with the back of her hand. "Life is like this stew I'm making. Some of the things in it are bitter, but you need them to give it body and flavor. Once everything gets worked in together, it all turns out just fine."

"Thank you, Martha, for your hospitality and your wisdom. It has been an honor to visit with you."

She nodded and went back to her stew.

Almost instantly Jen was back with total recall. She described the huge fireplace with a wrought iron swinging arm suspending a giant soup kettle over the coals.

"Have you ever heard of Lynne, Massachusetts? Do you think it could have been a real place?" she asked.

"I have no idea. As a healer, my focus is on the energy of the events and how they affect us in this lifetime."

"Oh, my," she broke in, "it's so dark! What time is it? We must have been away more than two hours." She reached for her purse.

I retrieved her coat and off she went. If she had lingered as long as she wanted, Jen would have been a seriously sleep deprived PR lady. Back to a semblance of reality, I puzzled a bit about that colonial woman. I hadn't the faintest clue how her story could be relevant in Jen's whirlwind New York City life. Suddenly overcome with voracious hunger, I grabbed a slice of pizza, threw together a salad and wolfed it down. This work burns up a lot of energy.

Mary Blake

Now to address that situation in California. Reality! Sigh.

Once family matters were under control, Martha's off-the-wall comment kept replaying in my head. Too exhausted to meditate, I programmed my unconscious to work on it with Spirit while I slept and crashed.

The next morning, I woke with an "aha." Martha had never been told intra-incarnational empathy couldn't work. She was so open to the core consciousness that Jen and she were on the same wavelength. That's probably why she just "knew" how Jen felt. Sometimes knowing is enough.

Chapter Nine
Voyaging as Spectator Sport

Don considered himself the godfather of the class. An eager student of metaphysics, he was intrigued when he learned about our extraordinary trips into other lifetimes. Though the mysteries of life after life fascinated him, he unashamedly confessed he was chicken. On the other hand, he was so curious he could think of little else. No one ever accused him of being short of ideas. He ran his factory in New Jersey like a conjurer. I knew he'd come up with an interesting solution sooner or later. Sooner turned out to be 11:00 pm. My captain of industry sputtered with excitement as he outlined his brilliant plan. Determined to have his cake and eat it too, he had devised an ingenious compromise. He couldn't wait to tell me about his idea.

"I've got it, Mary," he chuckled. "I'll pay for the session. All you have to do is come up with a suitable volunteer who will let me sit in and ask questions."

"Up to me, huh," I groused. The first dozen or so people I approached were not willing to allow a stranger to watch while they were in such a vulnerable state. To them, it was an extremely private experience... no voyeurs allowed.

Then came our lucky break. Melanie, a friend from Science of Mind classes, and I bumped into each other in a coffee shop. To my surprise, as we caught up with each other's lives, she pelted me with questions. "What's this I hear about you taking people into other lifetimes? Is it anything like Past Life Regression? I've always wanted to do that, but I'm beyond broke."

"Whoa, Melanie," I countered, "slow down. First off, I don't see how you could think of what we're doing as past. Everything unfolds naturally like everyday life. It's all present tense and we're in control of what happens. When it's in the past you can't change anything… it's all over and done with, right? So I've begun to think of this work as soul voyages."

"That sounds even better. I just wish I could afford it."

"Tell ya what I'm gonna do, Melanie," I giggled and outlined Don's outrageous plan.

"I'll do it! I'll do it!" she exclaimed. "Where? When?"

"The where is easy—my apartment. As to when, I'll get back to the guy and let you know."

In a couple of phone calls we arranged to meet in three days.

They arrived almost simultaneously. Melanie immediately stretched out on the couch. She was almost exploding with excitement, but trying her best to appear nonchalant.

Don perched on the edge of a chair, looking as if he might take flight momentarily. He had asked and received Melanie's permission to record the session. Aiming his tape recorder at her, he pulled a notepad and pen from his attaché case and was ready for action.

"What have we gotten into," I wondered. "Will this actually work?" No answer forthcoming, there was nothing left but to begin. I instructed Don not to turn his tape recorder on until after Melanie had arrived at her time or place with no one listening to the tape to float away to some unknown time or place with no one to bring them back.

After the candles were lit I said a prayer and urged Melanie to resist all expectations and just let it flow naturally. Then, determined to prevent the kind of suffering Art had gone through, I added something new. Much to her surprise, she agreed to experience no pain. Don was puzzled too, but kept his promise to remain silent. Satisfied that she was well prepared, I began.

Spiritual development studies made it easy for Melanie to slip into altered consciousness. Already in light trance I heard myself tell her to float away to another time and place, another aspect of her Whole Self, and an event that was affecting her success and happiness here and now. After a few moments, her head began to move as if she was looking around. A nod told Don it was okay to turn on his tape recorder.

Now we had to discover where we were and what was going on. Praying Spirit would arrive soon and take over, I dove in. "Can you describe your surroundings?" I prompted.

The Reluctant Farmer

Her response was instantaneous. "Yes. I'm on a farm… a big farm."

"What kind of farm?"

"We plant crops…. corn mostly. I see trees, an orchard—an apple orchard. There are lots of trees around. I have a long white dress on and an apron, and high lace-up shoes. They're black; I'm white."

Don's eyes widened; the idea of an African American being white in another lifetime must never have occurred to him. He made a note and hunched forward, fascinated.

Melanie chattered away, enthusiastically describing the scene. "My hair is black. I have long bangs and a white cap that ties under the chin like a bonnet."

"How old are you?"

"Uh… 13 or 14. My name is Carolyn."

"What is your mother's name?"

"Helen. My father's name is Ogar[3]. He works on the farm… he owns the farm."

The way she said it sounded like it was a big deal.

"What's happening right now?" I asked.

"My mother is working inside the house now, doing the laundry. She washes clothes on an old washboard. She's working very hard. It's hot. It's summertime. I like the heat."

Her chatter was infectious and my errant mind went wandering. "She likes the heat. Winters must be very hard for the homeless," flitted through my mind. I struggled to keep up with the non-stop girl talk about whatever occurred to her.

"Where's Spirit when you need him," I thought.

At that very moment Spirit picked up the questioning, "Can you tell me what year it is?"

"July, 1891. The corn is about ready for harvest."

"Anything interesting happening in your life?"

"Hmph!"

Don grinned. We got the message—nothing interesting ever happened on that big farm.

"Let's go forward in time to an important event in your life, Carolyn," Spirit suggested. "Just go there automatically as I count to three. One… two… three."

I barely had time to nod reassuringly at Don, who was out of his depth again, before Carolyn continued.

Escape From The Farm

"I'm getting married to a tall black man. His name is Hector. My parents don't like it. I don't really know him very well. He's waiting at the door… waiting for me. He has on a dark brown jacket and

---

[3] *The first US birth recorded with the name Ogar was June 6, 1881. Less than five per year were born with that name from 1880 through 2015. Carolyn's father might have been an immigrant.*

dark pants that are too short… black boots… lace-up old boots. Parson Richfield is going to marry us. Then we're going to go and live in Sacramento. Hector builds railroads. He works on the tracks. They don't pay him very well."

"Why did you decide to marry him, Carolyn?" Spirit asked, finally managing to get a word in edgewise.

"To get away. I wanted to go away… to another place."

"I see."

Silence… Melanie's face registered marked changes as Spirit patiently waited.

"Where are you now, Carolyn?" he inquired.

"In California. In the valley… it's called Hidden Valley [4]."

"And you're making your home in Sacramento?"

"I guess so. I feel strange. I don't know what's going to happen. I'm not sure what I'm getting into."

"Let's move forward to the time when you are settled in your new home."

"I'm so unhappy. I had a party and no one came. No one will talk to me. I'm an outcast… a white woman married to a black man. It's awful! I can't stand it… I want out of here!"

"What are you doing now, Carolyn?"

"I'm opening the drawer looking for something. There's a gun in the drawer. I take it out. I'm looking around now, looking at the gun. I just feel numb… no feeling. I just want out!"

My stomach knotted in fear that the girl was about to commit suicide. "What would happen if…," then I chided myself for that instant of doubt.

"Carolyn, you needn't concern yourself with anything," Spirit assured her. "Let go and we will lift you away from all your pain, sadness and disappointment. Just float there in that mellow

---

[4] *Telseyville, in Hidden Valley Lake NW of Sacramento was first settled in 1840.*

between-time and rest. Let the compassion and wisdom of the universe nourish and heal you. Now please share some of that understanding with Melanie. Tell her what she needs to know. Give her more peace of mind and happiness."

Silence. It felt like a lot was happening subliminally in that profound silence.

Don looked up, disappointment flooding his features. He was far from ready for the session to end.

Then Melanie took a deep breath and sighed peacefully. Somehow her features shifted and reshaped, projecting a totally different personality. I could sense an air of petulant irritation.

Down on the Delta

"Can you please describe where you are now and tell us what's happening?" Spirit prompted.

"It's a big old wooden house, but inside it's beautiful… lots of dark wood. I'm in the living room now. There's a big, beautiful couch… a white couch with brown wood. There's fancy carving all around it. There are tables and a big mirror. I have on a long white gown now. It's like a plantation dress. There's a party.

"No, no, it's not a party any more. I'm just walking around in the living room with this white dress on… looking around at a great big mess. I think I'll go upstairs. The stairs are carpeted and there are pictures of men on the wall, different family portraits. I'm walking up the stairs, looking for something. I'm walking and walking. There are a lot of stairs. My dress is rustling as I climb the stairs. I like the dress. It's beautiful.

"I'm upstairs now, in a big bedroom. There's a white cover on the bed. There's white everywhere in the bedroom. Something happened to the party. I'm so disappointed. It was my graduation party. Everything's gone all wrong."

"Let's go backwards within your life to a happier time…" Spirit suggested.

After a brief moment of heavy breathing the tension eased. The worried expression melted into a frown of concentration.

"Please tell me where you are and what's happening," Spirit asked.

"I'm sitting at my writing desk, writing out invitations."

"Where do you live?"

"In a big house on the Mississippi Delta. The house is right on the river. I can see it from my window."

"What year is it?"

"1860."

"What is your name?"

"Chris. Oh! There's a steamboat passing by. Now I'm downstairs on the porch. Everybody's going down to see the boat. There's a lot of people… ladies with their parasols. They're waving at the people on the boat. It's making a lot of noise. There are smoke pipes and a paddle on the end. I'm tired of watching that. I'm going back in the house.

"I'm all alone in the great room. I've been trying on my white graduation dress. Now I sit back down at my desk. I'm writing, 'Dear John, come on the 24th. Don't be late!' Now I'm sealing the letter. I'm looking out the window thinking about tomorrow… thinking about my party."

Don scribbled madly, trying to keep up with this bubbling teenager bouncing through time.

"My mother's too old to have children now," she confided. "My brother's name is Braque. He lives with us and he goes to college. He's here at the party wearing a black suit. He's giving something to his girlfriend. Somebody's taking my hand, asking me to dance. He's very handsome. We're dancing a waltz." Melanie's body weaved a bit as Chris danced.

It was all I could do to keep the energy flowing. How we had gotten from invitation to party was beyond me.

Chris hummed a happy tune… then suddenly screamed, startling Don. He looked at me for reassurance. I nodded to assure him everything was under control.

Fire!

"Somebody comes in shooting…" Chris reported breathlessly, "Just busts right into the house. They're shouting fire! Oh, no! Everyone ran out. The musicians threw their instruments right on the floor and took off running."

"Chris, look around you," Spirit urges. "Someone is trying to reach out to you… to help."

"The Captain is running next to me," Melanie panted. "He's the captain of the boat. 'Come with me,' he says. He's trying to get me to go with him. I'm running down the street shouting. Now I'm on the riverfront. I look back. Our house is ablaze. When the men shot their guns into the ceiling they accidentally set it on fire. I'm still running, running," she panted.

"There's a boat on fire!" she shouts. "It's the captain's boat. The dock and everything is all engulfed in flames. The people on the boat are screaming.

"The captain is next to me. He's shaking and crying. He's so sad—crying and crying… 'Timmy, Timmy… my Timmy's on the boat!" That's the captain's little boy.

"Oh, it's so terrible! His wife was on the boat too. A lot of people were killed. They're all dead now."

My hand automatically reached out to comfort her in this dreadful tragedy.

Don sat shaking his head, knowing there was nothing he could do. He was not accustomed to feeling helpless.

Melanie's body shook a bit, as if Chris was trying to rid herself of the dust and smoke from the fire.

"Where are you now, Chris?" Spirit asked.

"I'm back in the house, just standing here. There wasn't anything I could do down at the dock. Everything was burnt.

"I've found my mother. She's not as bad as I thought. I walk over to her and put my head in her lap. I'm very tired now. I'm going to bed."

"How are you feeling, Chris?" Spirit inquires kindly.

"The fire and people running all over, and people getting hurt and dying made me afraid. When I got back up here our house was just awful. The chairs are knocked over; food all over the place; dishes are smashed. Helen! Helen! Helen is the maid," she explains. "Somebody call Helen!"

Her head swivels frantically from side to side. Then her right foot jerks several times, in a stamping motion.

"I look around and I'm so mad. Such a big mess! Look at my dress—it's all stained. I'm stamping my foot at Helen. Clean this up right away! 'Yessum,' she says, 'yessum.'

"A black man comes in. He works in our house. His name is Jimmy. He tells us a lot of people were killed. Like we didn't know.

"Helen's telling him to come over and help her right now. He's mad, but he goes ahead and gets a big container to put all the garbage in. I'm just standing here, all mad. Mother's upstairs sleeping. It's 9 o'clock in the morning. What am I supposed to do about all this? I'm disgusted! I can't stand this mess!" She sniffs a couple of times.

"I know what I'll do. I'm going to go shopping! I think I'll go to the stationer's."

Shopping as Therapy

Chris brightens up a bit at the prospect. "I'll just go upstairs and get my coat and call for my carriage. Helen, send someone down to the stables and have my carriage brought up! Why are they always so pokey slow?

"Now I'm getting into the carriage. The horse is black and very pretty. I like the sound as he clip clops along… clip clop, clip clop… it's very soothing."

Her body sways gracefully on the couch to the movement of the cart.

"Now I'm in the shop buying a lavender sachet, soap in a little purse, and a pen. There's candy and clothes, lots of things in the store."

"Thank you Mr. Roy," she chirped, reaching out as if handing something to him.

I glanced at Don. He looked as bored as I was with Chris's self-indulgence.

"Let's go forward in time to the very last day you're on this plane in the body of Chris." Spirit prompted.

Melanie's voice became thin and brittle, "I'm old, old, old. I'm a hundred. The children are the most important things in my life. I have five. I'm a great grandmother. I have eighteen great grandchildren."

"Tell me what is happening and how you're feeling on this, your last day on earth."

"My stomach hurts. I'm doubled over. Help me! Help me! I'm dying!" Melanie pants weakly.

"Didn't she promise there'd be no pain?" I wondered.

"Don't be frightened, I'm taking your pain away," Spirit soothed. "Melanie and I will lift your spirit out of your body, very, very gently. Chris, you're not dying… you're being born into a new spirit body. You're going on to another plane. There will be no more pain. Float up out of your body and you'll see… you won't be old any more. There'll be no more weakness and pain. There… that's a whole lot better."

Melanie's breathing eased instantly. Her contorted face relaxed into a beautiful smile.

Bye Bye Bad Karma

Centenarian Advice

Spirit switched gears so smoothly I almost didn't realize what was happening. "We have some unfinished business, Carolyn," he announced. "Come with me. Follow the shining light before you."

Don and I stared at each other in joint confusion at these words. Were there two Carolyns, or was this the same one we visited before?

"Carolyn, from where you are now," Spirit continued, "you can reconnect with your greater consciousness, its compassion and wisdom. Now you can simultaneously see Melanie and your incarnation as Chris. Think about how what happened to you affected her life and further, how the combined influence of those two lives is now affecting Melanie. Allow the ambition, anger and guilt that tormented you to fade away. Understanding the effect of that combined spiritual residue, what advice would you like to give Melanie?"

Don's eyes registered a combination of amazement and the beginning of comprehension.

"Don't be so impatient, Melanie," Carolyn advised. "Laugh. Be good, and honest, and fair."

Chris chimed in, "Care for your loved ones. Work hard. Mind your own business."

Carolyn and Chris were both eager to depart. Spirit obliged.

I glanced over my shoulder at Don. He was having the time of his life, gesturing in circles to keep going—keep going! If Melanie and Spirit were willing, why not. I was beginning to get used to traveling through time and space, never knowing where we would land or who we would meet. The constantly expanding scope of the work was dizzying, but the breakthroughs were exhilarating!

Don handed me a much-needed glass of water. My throat was parched. I had no idea what might happen next. It all depended on Spirit.

Patient and indefatigable as usual, Spirit continued as if there had been no interruption. "Let's search further till we arrive at the origin of Melanie's, Chris's and Carolyn's impatience and anger. Float further and further away, to a time when anger was a way of life."

A Disastrous Sea Voyage

"Yes… yes…" Melanie's voice deepened in timbre and became harsh, urgent. "I see men below. I'll move in closer. Why, they're Vikings! There are five ships sailing into the dark. The men are so furious. They want to kill king Ursul. He's very cruel—he kills people who won't do what he wants them to do."

Don sat bolt upright on the edge of his chair. The transformation shocked him into rapt attention. The girl on my couch now emanated a very powerful male energy. He shook his head as if trying to make sense of it.

"Can you connect with anyone in or near these ships?" prompted Spirit.

"I'm on one of the Viking boats. All my men are around me."

"What is your name?"

"My name is Pieter."

"Tell us about yourself."

"I'm strong and I'm going out to kill. That's what I do."

"What's happening right now?"

"I'm freezing, but I like being cold. I love to feel the wind in my face. They're all hungry for battle. Everyone's shouting *Oopsagamee*—kill!—*Lang inshen*—right… turn right. The boats are all turning right."

At Thor's Command

"Can you tell me what year this is?" Spirit inquired.

Bye Bye Bad Karma

"The eleventh year of our Lord Thor. Thor commands me."

Don couldn't hold back a minute longer. "Is it all right if I ask a question?" he blurted.

"You may," Spirit assured him.

"How many years has it been between your time and my time?" he asked.

"4,000 years."

That was more than enough to impress Don. He had the look of a man who was really getting his money's worth.

"What country is this?" Spirit prompted.

"Kinsha. We sail towards the rising sun."

The Viking went on, reporting everything as it happened. "Our ships are approaching the city. There's war here. We're fighting the Yak.[5]"

---

[5] *Research revealed an ancient tribe called "people of the yak." "(sic}...the Longshan Culture of the late New Stone Age (2,800 - 2,300 B.C.)" (Qian Yanwen, 1979). The history of China's yak industry is thus at least 4,500 years old.*

A grunt, heavy breathing, then his voice resumed through gritted teeth.

"My heart hurts. Our ship was rammed. I fell down and hit my head. The people on that other boat are all over our ship. They have dark skins. I don't like them. They look evil. They look terrible. They're wearing long hats with a spike on the top. They don't have any shirts on. They have knives and they're cutting everybody up. One is jumping around waving my friend's head in the air. Now they're going to cut me."

"You will not experience any pain, Pieter. We are going to lift your soul out of that broken body. Now you're floating above the ship. Tell us what is happening now."

Silence.

"Pieter, your soul sister, Melanie, is reaching out to discover the connection between the two of you. Reach back to her, feel her soul and yours combine. What is happening to you affects her life too. She needs your help!"

"She is a woman. I don't like her. I will have nothing to do with her. We are taught not to have anything to do with women. Their affairs are their own."

Always adaptable, Spirit shifted the line of questioning, "What did you learn from your life?"

"How to kill."

I shivered. Don swallowed. Spirit, apparently unmoved, continued. "Come to think of it," I thought, "Spirit must have seen everything we could imagine and even more. He handles everyone and every situation flawlessly, no matter how unusual."

Transmutation of a Viking Soul

"Pieter, there are many things that are more powerful than killing. I want you to float far away from the body you just called your own. Reach out toward your higher self. Expand and become more in harmony with your soul purpose. Open to the greatness of the spirit you really are. Now give yourself the joy of receiving love for the first time."

"A big wave of love," Pieter sighed.

Don relaxed and took a deep breath himself in an effort to stay calm in the wake of these revelations.

"Share that big wave of love with Melanie," Spirit suggested. "Let it heal the both of you."

Heart melting vibrations filled the room, transforming Melanie's features.

"Now, speaking from that wave of tender compassion," Spirit urged, "help her in any way you can. Tell her what she needs to know."

"Don't be a fool. Stop running around and playing all the time. Have children—weave—tend the hearth. Be good to your husband."

Melanie's face was a sight to see!

"Thanks, Pieter," Spirit continued, "now let go of your smallness, your Earth limitations. Open more deeply to the spiritual wisdom unfurling around you. Let it expand far beyond the limited 'facts of life' you thought you knew," Spirit intoned. "Let the knowledge of the ages heal and nourish your soul. This more valid, universal truth is yours to take. I'm going to count to five. When I reach five you will have absorbed all the knowledge you need for this moment in time. One, two, three—it's getting clearer… Four… it's before, behind and beyond you… Five… you can see the pattern, the web. Pieter, with this new understanding, reach out to Melanie in any way you can. Are you willing to work with her now?"

Silence… then, with a huge sigh, Melanie seemed to melt into the couch. Her face underwent many changes, each more blissful, serene and relaxed than the last. Again and again she sighed, then stirred gently.

Spirit waited in silent observation mode. Don sat vigilant, clutching his notepad, impatiently waiting for more.

Instant Debriefing

"Melanie?" I asked hesitantly, "are you here?"

"Yes," she responded in her normal voice.

Don let out a sigh of disappointment. He obviously didn't want the session to end.

"Where is Pieter now, Melanie?" Spirit delicately inquired.

I caught my breath. Spirit had never spoken directly to any client after their return to current reality.

"Pieter is gone and I'm glad." Melanie responded. She didn't seem the least bit surprised to be conversing with Spirit.

"Do you understand what happened to Pieter's spirit and how it affected you?" Spirit continued.

"No. All I know is I feel better."

"Pieter was a child of a very warlike society. He lived to fight, to kill and to win… and died in battle against a superior force. His life of violence prevented him from enjoying peaceful endeavors… a family, love, children, community. Does that make sense to you?"

Melanie nodded thoughtfully.

"Think about what his world was like," Spirit continued, even more kindly and patiently than usual. "The societal rules his parents, teachers and fighting crew lived by are very different from that which you accept as truth, is that not so?"

"Yes."

"Was he angry when he left the Earth plane?"

"No, his spirit evolved," she responded.

"Before we helped him work out his karma, Pieter died at the hands of an enemy with dark skin, right?"

"Yes."

Don scribbled frantically, completely absorbed in this evolutionary lecture.

"Doesn't this explain why you chose to come back as an African American?" Spirit asked. "Think a moment. Pieter needed your help to heal his hatred of dark-skinned people. Can you accept his thank you gift now?"

"Yes."

Having thus challenged Melanie to acknowledge the lesson, Spirit quietly disappeared.

After a few moments of intense concentration, Melanie stretched, opened one eye and sighed. Then she sat up, gathered herself together, mumbled a brief goodbye and vanished into the night.

Don stared at me in puzzlement. "What did the Viking say?"

"I don't know. It was private between them, but by her reaction, it must have been very meaningful. If I had to guess, I'd say it was probably something about how brave she was to choose to incarnate as a black woman."

Don nodded thoughtfully, working this through in his mind. Before heading home to New Jersey, he thanked me profusely, paid for the session and requested another one in the very near future… like next week.

"It's up to Melanie," I countered, "If it's okay with her, it's fine with me."

Triangular Vibrations

Don's request for a second session was a surprise. If he was motivated by curiosity alone, that triple-header should have been the end of it. Perhaps he, too, felt there was more to learn from Melanie's unresolved karmic issues.

Melanie's three incarnations, so different and yet so strangely connected, haunted me. I searched my memories for insights into Spirit's reasons for choosing to visit those three very different lifetimes in one session. It was hard to see what they had in common. On the contrary, each aspect would have had a difficult time dealing with the other two.

Spirit's gift left Melanie with more unanswered questions than clarity. Instead of a simple solution, she had been given a challenge: think it through. The only connections I could think of between those three incarnations were anger and resentment. The uncontrollable temper that had cast such a pall on these three, and who knows how many other lives, had to be karmic. Was Carolyn and Chris's irritable nature a residue from the Viking's hate-driven life?

It was a very treacherous emotional pathway to unwind. The vibrations from the Viking's death at the hands of dark-skinned people had persisted for 4,000 years. Now it was up to Melanie to make peace with that hatred and rage. I wondered how she would fare in her challenge to master three disturbing karmic encounters with dark skinned people. Hopefully she would be able to resolve the hatred and rage that drove her Viking incarnation to his death. Was what she had learned from those three life stories sufficient to pull off a miracle and use it to master her current life issues? Could she do it without professional guidance?

Once again, Spirit had given a "previous incarnation," a chance to view Earth affairs from a different perspective. The different ways anger affected these three lifetimes illustrated the power of bad karma to impact on our happiness and success in any lifetime.

What a rare opportunity to learn, to grow, and to observe the power of free will in action. The vast potential of the work that was unfolding hit me like a sledgehammer. More than ever, I was convinced that karma is just a shadow compared to the potential of an enlightened human spirit.

Chapter Ten
Never on Sunday

Jen called with a surprising revelation. At first she half suspected it might be an illusory experience. After her visit to the colonies she did some research and found there was a town in Massachusetts named Lynne that dated back to the mid 17th century. That bit of corroborative evidence eliminated any skepticism as to the validity of her experience.

Over the next few weeks Jen's sharp edge seemed to mellow a bit. After class one evening she confided, "As lovely as Martha was, the original purpose behind my foray into another lifetime wasn't even touched upon, much less resolved."

"Umm," I mused, "perhaps it was necessary to deal with that lifetime before we tackled something major."

"Sounds ominous, but let's go for it," she shot back. "I guess sooner than later would be best." We agreed on a time for the follow-up session and Jen headed home.

As we began the relaxation process, Spirit was already on hand. That was surprising. So was the request for Jen to agree that she would experience no pain whatsoever. The emphasis seemed unusually heavy. She solemnly gave her word.

In record time she was on her way to the time and place selected by her Whole Self. As we neared the chosen destination she exclaimed, "It's Greece… more primitive than I remember, but definitely Greece!"

Primitive? My first guess was the biblical era. "Not a good sign that this will be a routine trip," I mused. My left hemisphere was off in an attempt to find the link between this Greek existence and Jen's present life. She seemed to have a "thing" against organized religion. Whenever the subject came up, she'd offhandedly remark that it legitimatized small-minded people's prejudices.

"Notice your surroundings and describe them, please," Spirit instructed.

"Wouldn't it be ironic if she landed in a religious community," I thought irreverently, then caught myself and concentrated on getting out of the way.

As her observation of the surroundings sharpened, it became clear that my speculation was way off mark.

"It's not a nice neighborhood, that's for sure," Jen stuttered. "Ugh! It's squalid, and the people are… not respectable."

"There's another aspect of your Whole Self nearby. Seek that person out," Spirit prompted.

A Dark Beauty

With a look of absolute disbelief, she gasped, "Oh, no, that can't be any relation to me!"

"Look closer," Spirit advised.

"How can that curvaceous young brunette with a head-and-a-half of unruly black curls be connected to me?" Jen muttered.

I listened, fascinated. This was way beyond my skill level.

Spirit gently but firmly drew Jen on until she finally had to admit this could be the incarnation she sought to resolve her unspoken dilemma. That might explain why this soul sister was so different from the modest, self-effacing colonist.

"Speak to her," Spirit prompted.

When hailed, the woman paused reluctantly, shrinking into a niche between the buildings. Thinking a female voice might reassure her, I introduced myself and asked who she was… and where we were.

In a frightened whisper she told us her name… "I'm Lyrika. Please, I must hide! I must find shelter or they'll find me."

Bye Bye Bad Karma

A psychic impression of harsh voices and pounding feet told me it was too late. Lyrika's pursuers had caught up with her.

But why was this charming young woman being chased down like a criminal? "Instant knowing" told me a local taboo had been broken—probably sexual. My left hemisphere was reeling. The Jen I knew was all business, not even remotely sexually provocative.

They dragged Lyrika through back alleys and threw her into a dark, dank cell. Jen was in a state of shock.

"What historic timeline is this, anyway," I mused in my little corner of consciousness.

Jen squirmed on the couch. What an effort it must have been for her to admit the slightest affinity toward such a lifestyle… in any incarnation. The scenario seemed painfully illogical. I reached out to comfort her but she jerked away at my tentative touch.

Lyrika was understandably suspicious, but finally allowed me to comfort her as best I could. I stroked Jen's forehead and stomach, which eased her violent trembling somewhat.

Spirit assured her that whatever she had done, we were here to help. "Please tell us what's gone wrong so we'll know how to help." Gentle questioning finally broke through her shame and mortification.

"A married man seduced me and we had an affair," she mumbled between racking sobs.

"…And the man is judged innocent, bearing no guilt in the matter," Spirit finished for her. His voice, though compassionate, confirmed awareness of local mores. The right of men to take and use women who "tempted" them was beyond question.

Jen was outraged. That antiquated version of justice was a foreign concept to this 20th century career woman. "We've got to help her," she gasped.

"Sadly, she can't allow us to help her now," Spirit calmly announced.

Mary Blake

Mob Frenzy

We watched in horror as the mob overtook her, beat her into submission and dragged her away. Spirit and I were a silent, invisible support team as Lyrika was forced to endure the ridiculous parody of a trial. She was permitted no defense during a dramatic recitation of her wanton criminal acts, primarily adultery and destruction of a fine citizen's good name and reputation. Within minutes the farcical trial was over. The list of heinous cruelties to be inflicted upon her seemed endless. I caught my breath in horror at the sentence. The "good people" were not satisfied to just kill her. Extreme punishment was recommended.

She was transferred to a filthy, primitive cell to await her punishment. I prayed Jen would be strong enough to deal with this savagery.

"Float high above and simply observe," Spirit commanded. "You need not suffer for even a moment. The knowledge of the situation is all that is necessary."

Fully aware of the blessing she'd just received, Jen quickly floated above the scene. She was definitely not the martyr type. If there were even a slim chance to avoid suffering the agony of torture and dismemberment, she'd gladly take it.

My heart swelled with gratitude for Spirit's reminder of her agreement that there would be no pain. I made a note to make an agreement for pain-free sessions a primary rule.

Bye Bye Bad Karma

Reporter at Large

From her bird's-eye view above the frenzied mob, Jen assumed the role of on-the-scene reporter, describing the inhuman torture in detail. "Lyrika's mangled body is being displayed as a warning to future adulteresses," she reported.

Then after a brief silence she continued grimly, "I guess the novelty wore off. Now they're hacking her body to pieces and throwing it piece by piece into the street. Oh, God," she moaned. "A dog is running down the street with one of her hands in its mouth!"

I was trembling, struggling desperately not to interfere with the process.

Jen had had it, "Haven't we learned enough?" she cried.

Apparently we had. Spirit issued explicit instructions for Jen to go to her most perfect vacation place to recuperate in the 20th century. Instantly she was in a serene, nourishing environment greedily soaking up healing energy. After that well-earned virtual vacation, she floated back into her body.

Back to so-called normal, a rejuvenated but badly shaken former cynic groaned, "Christ! Why couldn't we have had one of those past life regressions the critics always claim we're about, where everyone is a king or a queen, or a famous general or something?"

"I know, what a shock! After that lovely first trip, I never expected an evening of high drama. Guess I should have known better," I sighed.

As we wobbled our way to the door, she gasped, "At least no one can accuse us of inventing an ego-flattering fantasy world. I'm on my knees! How am I going to get home?"

"A taxi?" I offered hesitantly, only half joking. After such a grueling session, I was genuinely concerned.

"A taxi for five blocks? Why not!" She almost managed a grin.

She staggered out half-dazed and I prayed she'd get home safely after that living nightmare.

As for me, thank God I didn't have to go anywhere. I was lucky to manage to put out the candles and crawl into bed… no time or energy for evaluation or recapitulation. I was asleep almost before I felt the sheet under me.

Post Mortem

The following evening Jen called to talk it through and hopefully to put the Lyrica connection in perspective. "This is something I've never told anybody," she confided. "Would you believe I was in an 11-year marriage that was only consummated six times? And I'm a Scorpio! Could that Greek tragedy be the key to my almost total disinterest in sex?"

That rare confidential disclosure underscored the karmic relevance of that session. "In light of the horrors we witnessed, that makes total sense," I agreed. "Sexual abuse buried so deeply resonates through many lifetimes with disastrous consequence. According to Spirit, you had to witness this in order to work through your subconscious blocks and live a more normal life."

"Well, I don't know about my subconscious or whatever, but for sure it's still resonating through my conscious mind," she quipped.

"I'm sure this information was given you for a very good reason. Spirit would never have allowed you to witness this if it wasn't vitally important for you to know and understand. You have plenty of time to process this knowledge into wisdom. With your ability to recognize the irrational conclusions of the past, you can work it through and resolve the issue, I know. It's just a matter of time. Right now, let's both get a good night's sleep, hopefully without nightmares about righteousness run amok, and monstrous atrocities at the hands of the great unwashed."

"Thanks, I can give it a try," she sighed and hung up.

Chapter Eleven
Three Crazy Guys

The forecast was cold and colder. I couldn't imagine anyone would show up for our class, but Jen and Elizabeth braved the snow to attend class. It felt like an omen to me. As they gratefully sipped mugs of hot tea, I prayed for inspiration. My Number One Guide, Stardust, didn't fail me.

"Anyone who shows up for class in weather like this deserves something special... totally different," I smiled. "Let's hold hands and see if we can astral project together into a lifetime in which the three of us knew each other."

Shining eyes and bobbing heads registered their joint enthusiastic approval of this novel idea.

We joined hands and repeated the class affirmation. As the energy built, I asked that we three be taken to another place, another time in which we were all together.

We bounced around a bit. Evidently, we three had known each other in many different eras. Glimpses of some of them flashed by —a primordial jungle, an ice forest, then Elizabeth cried enthusiastically, "Oh, Greece! Let's go!"

"No, no, no! Not Greece!" Jen shrieked. "Once was more than too much!"

Something Special

With a jolting thud the PR executive, the comptroller of a major New York hospital and their disoriented spiritual teacher landed solidly into sweaty male bodies astride even sweatier horses. Man was it hot! The only other time I'd experienced heat like that was in

Mary Blake

Gila Bend, Arizona, where it was 125º Fahrenheit at noon.

Now it was my turn to recoil in horror. Oh, how we stank! How long had it been between baths? "Why, of all places, did we have to land in such miserable heat?" I wondered. Born with zero heat tolerance in a place called "Little Egypt," I had almost died of heat at age one. Sunstrokes and heat prostration plagued me all my life.

I longed for a way to steer us anywhere else. No luck; I was stuck! Leaders can't cop out.

With bewildering certainty, we all knew precisely where, when and who we were. It was 1848 and we were "gringos" on the way home from the Mexican American War. We joked and carried on as only war buddies can. Roy was the joker, Jack the tough guy and Mac (me) a medic.

"A healer again. How surprising," I thought.

Bye Bye Bad Karma

The joke du jour was, "Where'd you get that hat, Roy?" Our jokester sported a huge Mexican hat, complete with bobbing pom-poms, which almost obscured his whole head. We slapped our thighs, laughing uproariously at our own jokes. In this mood of high hilarity, we vied for the most outrageous things conquering heroes could do back home.

We came up with a crazy scheme to break away from the rest of the company and take a shortcut across Texas. Home seemed closer every minute.

"Imagine us just settin' there in the front porch swing with a tall cold drink, hooting and hollering whilst the rest of the boys struggle in... dusty, wore out, ragged and dyin' a'thirst," Roy crowed. We congratulated ourselves on our cleverness.

All Gone Wrong

Our grand plan didn't take long to go awry. We three jokesters got lost in the desert.[6] All too soon we ran out of food. Then, canteens empty, we stumbled across an arroyo. The horses charged forward and lapped up the deposits of rusty-colored stagnant water. Within seconds they were writhing in agonizing convulsions, beyond help of any kind. With a dull sense of imminent doom, each us shot our own horse.

Without horses or water we couldn't hope to last much longer. Exhausted, sunburnt, dehydrated, and half starved, we stared at the only water within miles—water that had just poisoned our horses.

The huge Mexican hat that had entertained us so protected Roy from the worst of it. Jack and I were blistered beyond bearing. As we sank weakly onto the sand Roy purposefully strode into the stream, dipped his hat into the water and slapped it on his head.

"Hold on, fellas," he muttered, "I got an idea. This stream has

---

[6] *According to the map of Texas, this apparently was the Chihuahua Desert.*

got to go somewhere. I'm goin' for help. I'll be back to getcha. Just don't die on me!"

Dripping foul water, Roy doggedly trudged downstream.

"Roy's gonna make it, I know he will, Jack muttered hoarsely. He lay helpless on the burning sand. "I can't hold out much longer," he gasped.

I lay on my left side, in fetal position.

The scene was vividly real. Jack and I experienced it together moment by moment. Roy had disappeared into the distance.

Rattler!

A rattlesnake slithered onto my leg and perched on my right knee. "Jack," I mumbled deliriously, "I got this great idea. If we can catch this thing we can kill it and eat it."

"Too late…I'm going…" Jack whispered with his last breath.

The snake coiled to strike. Eyes distended, sparkling like black diamonds, it swayed hypnotically, mesmerizing me. Lightning fast, it struck my thigh. Death was instantaneous.

Our hands loosened and we snapped back 133 years to New York, January 1981. We stared at each other, frozen between awe and overwhelm. Then Jen and Elizabeth swiped at sweat and gasped for a drink. I wobbled to the refrigerator and slopped cold water into three glasses. Gulping thirstily, we struggled to describe our individual experience.

Ad Hoc Epiphany

We three had been great pals, yes; all male, yes; on the way home from the war, yes; lost in a Texas desert… yes! Every indelible detail coincided perfectly.

We grabbed each other and hung on wordlessly… struggling to adapt the lingering energy from that incredible experience into a new concept of life, space, time and reality. Almost simultaneously we gasped, "Have three people ever done anything like this before?" We stared at each other, bereft of certainty save the triply-confirmed realization that we had all been given an extraordinary gift.

"Enough!" I said. "Maybe a good night's sleep will help us sort it through."

In a fog of emotional overwhelm, Jen and Elizabeth struggled into their winter coats and staggered toward the door. With nothing left to say, we hugged fiercely, like long-lost brothers.

Eventually the enigma of those crazy cowboys slipped through the rabbit hole to wherever impenetrable mysteries go und we gave up trying to make sense of an unforgettable, unfathomable event.

Chapter Twelve
Two for the Money

Don called to invite me to dinner. The session with Melanie was all he could talk about. After reading and re-reading his notes, and listening to the recording many times, he still had more questions than answers. He just couldn't understand how "past" incarnations could work outside the law of genetics. It didn't seem logical to him that a soul might have the ability to leap from race to race and male to female. "It's bugging me," he confessed, "I just can't get it through my head what kind of paradigm these incarnations work from. I think we ought to continue the experiment to see if there is any kind of pattern that we have overlooked."

"I know what you mean, Don," I responded. "It's hard to analyze. There seem to be two separate, overlapping themes in those three lifetimes—the racial issue and rage."

"I never thought about that," he mused. "I think you might be right."

The Elusive Thread

"Okay, don't forget we started out by asking that she be taken to another lifetime where something was happening that interfered with her current happiness and success. Both of those issues are obviously affecting Melanie on an ongoing basis.

"Spirit always seems to home in on the serious purpose behind each visit," I continued. "Let's see if we can discover the connection. The two female lifetimes, so close on the timeline, were obviously about racial issues. On the other hand, it was hard to see what Melanie had in common with a violent, anger-driven fighting machine. Then it hit me: Pieter's uncontrolled anger had held sway in all three lifetimes. Carolyn's resentment and depression might have derived from unexpressed anger. Chris had quite a temper too. Also, the people who killed Pieter had dark skins!"

Don nodded thoughtfully. "That makes me more excited than ever to have another go at it. See if you can get hold of her and set it up, okay? I'll take care of your fee, just like last time."

I agreed but hoped he wouldn't be disappointed. I realized there was no way to plan ahead. I did wonder if we would visit more than one interconnected lifetime again. The thought gave me shivers.

When I ran into Melanie she was practically delirious at the prospect of another "free cosmic ticket through time."

On the agreed-upon day for round two I took extra care with preparations. Candles, incense and music—everything was ready. Arriving with his usual precision timing, Don seemed even more wound up than usual. It was good we had a chance to mellow out with a cup of herbal tea.

The Big One

"I've got a feeling this is going to be really big… I mean even bigger than last time," he confided. "I think she's going to go very, very deep this time," he predicted, waving both arms expansively.

"I have no idea… as usual," I smiled.

Don went over his notes from the first session again while we waited.

Melanie arrived, aglow with anticipation. Almost exploding with excitement, she handed me a small packet of drawings. "This is the dress I was wearing and some of the furniture in the great room," she announced.

Don and I looked at the drawings with amazement. How detailed they were!

Bye Bye Bad Karma

"I couldn't sleep for days I was so excited," she sang out. "Can we start right away?"

With such enthusiastic participants, there was no point to delay. The room crackled with excitement. "What if nothing happens," I wondered, then canceled the thought. "Calm down. Follow your own advice; don't think," I told myself, then pleaded silently, "Oh, Spirit, please don't let us down!"

Melanie had already settled herself on the couch and was relaxing with deep breathing. I touched in with her to guide her into an altered state of consciousness. At warp speed she slipped into another somewhere.

"Can you describe where you are and what's happening?" I asked.

"Um, I'm going back and forth, back and forth, back and forth," came a very un-Melanie girlish singsong chant.

Don looked at me with a worried expression. Now it was he who was having doubts.

"Back and forth between what… where?" I prompted in an attempt to catch up.

"First I'm in an old, old town," Melanie reported. "I see a castle… but then everything changes and there's this western town… the Old West. The castle is gone and I've got a gun fastened against my side. I'm walking down a dusty road in this western town. Um, she sang… now I'm back at the castle and now I'm back in Texas. I'm bouncing… floating… I keep on bouncing back and forth between the castle and that dusty road in that dusty little town."

Don looked as if he was going to levitate. He fumbled with his tape recorder, hit record and held himself in check with considerable effort.

Spirit popped in and deftly rescued me, "Let's visit the castle first. When we're finished there we can go to that little town in Texas."

"That's a good idea. I like the castle," Melanie cooed. Her voice sounded strikingly different and the words came out subtly altered.

"Is that a bit of an accent? Wonder of wonders," I thought. Finally able to breathe, I slipped into observation mode in some corner of my mind and settled down to funnel energy and watch the show. What a relief!

"Order your bubble to float above the castle and tell us what it looks like up close," Spirit instructed.

I couldn't help speculating, "Is she on a tour to visit European castles—a student, an archaeologist? Fascinating!"

"Okay, there's four towers," she announced, tour guide fashion, "look-out towers… one on each corner. It's made of grey stone. The walls are really thick in some places and not so thick in others. There's a ditch around it and a bridge over it that's on a kind of pulley thing. The water's all muddy and filthy. Huh!" she huffed in exasperation, "I thought castles were supposed to be glamorous."

"What else can you see from outside the castle?" Spirit prompted.

"There are guards with pointed silver hats wearing red vests with a gold eagle. This is the fourteen hundreds," she stated emphatically.

"Float into the castle," our guide encouraged, "and look around till you find the other aspect of your Whole Self who lives here."

A Princess and Her Castle

"There's a princess walking down the stairs of the castle. I see her! She's a redhead with blue eyes and very, very pale skin… and (gasp) I am the princess! I have my crown on. My name is Anne—Princess Anne. I'm fifteen years old. My castle is Hindenberg. My father's name is Karl Eisel Strensen. We live in Elderberg, Germany… er, Holterberg. In the morning I get up and go to my tutor and talk about Greek and Latin. I study a lot. I study astrology with a very learned man. My tutor's name is Sir Longley. I do embroidery…

tapestry, and I frame it. I play the lute. I like to cook pheasant. I put it in the big stone oven and mix it with apples and a new spice one of our men brought back from Tarragona. It's quite expensive but we can afford it. I have very few friends. My best friend is named Suzanne." She prattled away like a typical teenager.

"Let's go forward in time to the next important thing that happens to you, Princess Anne," Spirit interrupted gently.

"Ooh! We're being invaded! Vandals! They're climbing over the walls, smashing things. They've got my mother! My father throws himself at them trying to rescue her." She screams, "They've smashed his head in with a club. My tutor has grabbed me, mussed me up and threw a dirty old rag over me. He's found a napkin and is tying it over my head and shoving me down in a corner by the pantry. I'm terrified, but he puts his hand over my mouth and tells me to be still as death if I know what's good for me. If any stranger comes up to me I'm supposed to speak to him in Gaelic."

"How do you happen to know Gaelic?"

"My teacher speaks Gaelic," she whispers.

"Melanie, take your bubble forward in time," Spirit prompted, "to the next important event that happens to Princess Anne."

A gentle shiver passed through her body. She seemed to stop breathing. Then the trembling stopped abruptly and she lay very still.

"Princess Anne?" Spirit ventured.

Queen Anne

"You'll address me as Queen Anne, thank you," came the haughty response.

"How long have you been queen?" Spirit inquired.

"My father and mother were killed in a foray against the castle and there's only me now."

"That just doesn't compute!" my errant thoughts insisted.

"Melanie is homeless, living with house squatters in a very dangerous area on the Lower East Side. She's never shown signs of grandiose pretensions, but she seems to be taking it all in stride. Where is this coming from?"

Ignoring my intrusion, Spirit continued quite seriously, "What about the people who attacked your castle? Are they still giving you trouble?"

"No, they were mad at my father, not at me."

"I see… and now it's all on your shoulders. How does it feel to be Queen?"

"Terrible!" she spat, "I have to sign proclamations all day long and hear endless complaints… and I can't pay the bills because nobody pays their taxes. And how am I supposed to fix the hole in the roof if nobody's paying taxes? And it's raining… it's raining right on my proclamations!"

Don coughed discreetly in an effort to suppress shock or amusement (perhaps a bit of both) at her queenly complaints. It tickled my funny bone too.

"You've done a fine job, Queen Anne," Spirit commented. "It looks as if you've learned valuable lessons. Wealth and prestige are not nearly as important as the people we love. You've taken on a great deal of responsibility. It's no small matter to step up and take the reins in the midst of such tragedy. You can be very proud of yourself."

Queen Anne smiled, acknowledging the compliment with a royal nod.

Taking that as our dismissal, Spirit calmly announced, "I think we're ready to visit that little dusty town in Texas, Melanie. Just order your bubble to take you there right now."

We waited, suspended in time.

On the Happiness Trail

Melanie squirmed a bit and appeared to grow a couple of inches. Don held his breath as the moments passed.

Spirit seemed to be taking time out too, so I succumbed to curiosity and spoke up tentatively. "Hello, my name is Mary, who am I speaking with?"

"Mah name is Te-ex," he answered. Melanie's voice morphed into a musical baritone. His name, rolling out in two syllables, sounded like something out of a cowboy song.

"What are you doing Tex?" I queried.

"Jist a'walkin' along, right on down the road," he drawled.

"Where are you headed?"

"We-ell, ah just got back from runnin' a buncha cows down to South Texas and ah got me a mighty thirst. Ah'm headin' fer that there saloon."

"What's the name of the saloon?"

"Sha-a-a-dy Lady!" he sang.

"Mind if I come along?" I asked.

"Fine with me. Ah go through the swingin' doors," Tex narrated. "Mah spurs are a'clinkin against the stone floor. Barkeep! Send over a bottle a' bourbon an' three glasses." Melanie's index finger stabbed the air, indicating where to place the glasses.

"Are you drinking with friends?"

"Ye-ep," he chuckled. "Me, mahself an' ah!"

"So tell me, Tex, are you married?" I asked.

"Nope, n' I ain't agonna be. Gittin' hitched is not fer me."

"How old are you, Tex?" was all I could think to ask.

"Fifty-six 'n goin' strong."

"What more can I say to a guy in a saloon with nothing on his mind except a bottle of bourbon?" I wondered.

Spirit glibly rescued me. "Let's go forward in time to the next important thing that happens to you, Tex," came the cosmic instructions.

"The stagecoach's a'rollin' inta town. Folks'r all in a termoil, like as usual," Tex remarked.

"How often does this happen?" Spirit encouraged the laconic Texan.

"Oh, 'bout onc't a month. Well, lordy, lordy… lookee here!" he sang out.

"What's happening, Tex?"

"We-ell, if'n you ain't the purttiest little filly I ever did see!" Tex crooned, ignoring us completely. "Allow me to he'p you down. Them steps is mighty steep fer a little gal like you."

If the big grin that lit Melanie's face was any indicator, our cowboy was totally smitten.

Once again, Spirit nudged us forward in time. Melanie squirmed a bit uncomfortably. The grin was replaced by a scowl.

For the Love of Annabelle

"What's happening, Tex?" Spirit prompted.

"I'm a'drownin' mah sorrows in some fine Texas bourbon."

"What's troubling you?"

"A pretty little lady from New England by th' name a' Annabelle."

"That sounds serious, Tex. Doesn't the lady return your affection?"

"Mah heart's plumb broke. She don't want nothin' to do with a grubby ol' cowpoke that's gone on cattle drives months at a time."

"Sounds like you need a different occupation."

"Don't know nothin' else. All I ever wuz wuz a trail hand."

"Is there anything else that's coming between you and Annabelle?" Spirit asked.

"Well, fer sure, there's no way I kin give her what she's usta… fancy things, a fine home. Them things takes money!"

"Did it ever occur to you that you have other ways of making money?"

"Huh?" Tex gulped, "Never heerd a'such!"

"Do you know those mountains off to the North, up toward the West end of the panhandle?"

"How does Spirit know so much about Texas geography," I wondered. A surprised grunt from Don indicated a similar reaction. Apparently Spirit was fully versed in mundane as well as spiritual matters.

"I know the very range you're talkin' about," Tex asserted.

"Did you ever think about trying your hand at prospecting? There's a very rich vein of silver in those hills. I can guide you," Spirit assured him.

"I'm already halfway there. Jist lemme saddle m'hoss," he babbled excitedly.

"Not just yet, Tex. I think you'll need some supplies… a burro and mining equipment. You must be well prepared for this venture," opined our remarkably resourceful guide.

"Lemme think on it a minute. I dunno about these thangs. Are you sure?"

"I have a very reliable source," Spirit assured him solemnly.

"Then ah'll do it!" Tex exclaimed. "There's an ol' codger hangs 'round the stables that claims he knows th' ropes. He's enertained us more'n wunst with his tall tales 'bout diggin' fer gold. 'Cordin' t'him it's back-breakin' work."

"Yes, of course," Spirit agreed, "but when you find what you're looking for, you won't have any trouble giving Annabelle the things she's accustomed to."

"Awrightee! How do I start?"

"First you must get permission to mine the area. Don't be surprised if some folks in town make fun of you and tell you you're off on a wild goose chase. If you really want to win Miss Annabelle you must get serious, believe in yourself and take action. You might have some mighty interesting dreams. Remember them and follow your guidance. Every hunch will bring you closer to your heart's desire."

Tex was as good as his word. He tracked down the "ol' codger" and pumped him for information. Then Spirit directed him through the beginning steps of the most important endeavor of his life. After a weighty silence, he suggested, "Now let's go to the next big event in your life."

The Silver Lining

"Welcome! Welcome to our happy home," Tex enthused. "And I'm a'gonna carry ya right acros't the threshold, just like in them fancy novels you're always a'readin.'"

Melanie's face revealed more than a thousand words could possibly convey. Obviously, the day-to-day details of Tex's struggle and triumph were none of our business.

The grin on Don's face told me how tickled he was that Tex had found his silver lining.

Spirit proceeded to take Tex through his new, amazingly improved life to a prosperous, peaceful ending. Surrounded by his loving family, Tex floated off toward Cowboy Heaven.

Spirit now addressed his newly released spirit. "Tex, before you head off to your heavenly reward, think a minute. You had a real fine life here thanks to Melanie. She brought you luck, right? Now it's your turn to do something for her. Just like you, she needs all the good advice she can get. Don't you think that might be a fair trade?"

"Yessir! I'll be happy to help the little lady out. Seems I owes her sumpin' for her part in this here adventure. Couldn't a'done it without her, it appears. Hmm, lemme think a bit. Now lissen here, Missy," he began gruffly, "ya gotta settle down, learn all ya can from them classes yer takin' an' make sompin' out'a yerself, y'hear? Learnin' ain't good fer nothin' lest ya mix it with grit, guts an' git

Bye Bye Bad Karma

'er done!"

Melanie gasped in surprise at that plainspoken advice.

"There's some spirits after me to move along," Tex continued, "but ah promise to look after ya as best as ah kin."

Spirit and Tex left with a whoosh. I stretched and breathed a sigh of relief. It gets a bit cramped in that bubble. Now it was time to finish my part of the job.

"Take a deep breath, Melanie and stretch," I began. "Soak up all that cowboy optimism and float back to New York City, to everyday life. Hold on to the happy feelings. Bring the confidence back with you. Be grateful that you have Tex as a spirit guide to help you conquer here and now. I'm sure he'll help you find a place to live and a way to support yourself."

Melanie followed instructions and then sat up, rubbed her eyes and yawned. "I feel wonderful," she sighed. "How long was I out?"

About three hours," Don volunteered, looking at his watch. "Oh, boy is it late! I didn't know we'd be so long. Can I give you a ride to wherever you need to go?"

Touched but obviously embarrassed, Melanie mumbled, "I'd hate for you to go there… it's an abandoned building on the Lower East Side."

Don, ever the gentleman, peeled off a fifty dollar bill and stuffed it in Melanie's pocket. "This'll take care of your taxi fare home. Come on young lady, let's go. It's getting later by the minute. Look at the candles… burned down to a stump! And I've got to get back to Jersey!"

Melanie, dignity intact, gathered her things and tucked the fifty into a safe place.

After hugs all around, they both left. Alone, I struggled to make sense of it all. The more I learn the less I know about these amazing trips into other lifetimes.

One thing for sure, Don's premonition was right. It had been a "big one." He had gotten even more than he hoped for. He had bought a ticket to observe someone else's trip into the unknown, knowing it might be a total bust. Instead, he got a triple header and then a double header. No wonder he was thrilled.

I, on the other hand, had even more than usual to sort out. Melanie had bounced back and forth between two lives centuries apart. Oh my! How were those two lifetimes connected? Maybe they had something to do with Melanie's financial plight. When we first met Princess Anne, money—lots of it—hadn't made her happy. Tex, on the other hand, was broke but carefree.

Spirit introduced new ideas and coached Tex in ambitious endeavors he never would have dreamed of on his own. I wondered if his newly-created wealth and the happiness it brought would inspire Melanie to change her attitude toward money. Only time would tell.

All I knew for sure was that bouncing back and forth between centuries and from Germanic mini-royalty to the roustabout world of that dusty town in Texas was hard work. I couldn't wait to hit the sack.

Chapter Thirteen
High Stakes and Burning Questions

Every new session probed deeper into unexplored layers of consciousness. I was learning the hard way how much expertise, awareness, empathy and respect is required to meet the karma-creating, pivotal events embedded in the core consciousness head-on. The unresolved conflicts we encounter and deal with often involve danger, pain and tragedy. When that happens Spirit takes over and works miracles that leave me breathless. More and more, this convinces me that the method employed in accessing "past lifetimes" can either resolve karmic issues or create new ones.

The best-known method to uncover memories of past lives, which our work is often confused with, is "past life regression." That method, which has been around since 1958, uses hypnosis to contact other incarnations. To understand how it works, I looked up the *Oxford Dictionary* definition of hypnosis: *"The induction of a state of consciousness in which a person loses the power of voluntary action and is highly responsive to suggestion or direction. Its use in therapy, typically to recover suppressed memories, or to allow modification of behavior by suggestion, has been revived but is still controversial."*

According to reliable sources, in hypnotic past life regression patients either observe or relive events exactly as they happened, complete with physical pain and emotional trauma. Since the past is over and done with, nothing can be changed. The perspectives gained might then be useful in ongoing traditional therapy.

In our sessions clients never surrender control. They choose to go into "another now," where something is happening that prevents or limits their happiness, success or wellbeing. They contact other incarnations, learn about their lives and help work through the issue(s) that created the bad karma. A powerful, wise Spirit presence protects, guides and advises clients, but never overrides their decisions or actions. After the session, they recall everything that had happened, often even more vividly than current events. After their session, clients usually report that they feel freer and more confident, more optimistic about their futures.

Popularity and enthusiasm for hypnotic past life regression continues to grow. Other than that failed regression in London, I had no evidence to support my concerns about the method. New evidence came all too soon, and from a most unexpected source.

Paul Maslow, younger brother of one of the founders of humanistic psychology, called to invite me to his healing circle. Much had happened since his days as brother Abe's favorite Rorschach test interpreter. Now in his seventies, he was a highly respected member of the metaphysical community. In addition to his own research, he maintained strong ties with top English healing practitioners. Paul was an expert in radionics and a founding member of the American Society of Dowsers.

Usually I'd have gladly accepted his invitation. Then he proceeded to enthusiastically announce, "I think you'll be very interested in meeting this man. He's one of the foremost experts in the field, a highly successful author and head of a prestigious psychological organization. He has done a great deal of research and work with private patients and he's going to give a demonstration. I know you won't want to miss it because he does the same thing you do."

"I didn't think anyone did the same thing I do!" I responded.

"Oh, yeah," he laughed, "past life regressions. He hypnotizes people and tells them where to go and they go right there."

"But Paul, that's not what I do."

"Oh, well, it's all the same thing. Apparently it's all very simple. He's even training a high school student to do it!"

As much as I respected Paul's intelligence, experience and generosity in sharing knowledge, something inside me screamed "No! This is wrong!" I took a breath and tried to find a polite way to refuse the invitation without offending my friend.

Offhand Comment or Prophecy?

"Paul, forgive me, but I couldn't possibly attend. I don't believe in hypnotizing people and telling them where to go. Next, I think it's incredibly irresponsible to teach this to a high school student. What if someone wound up being burned at the stake? How could a high school student, no matter how bright, possibly handle a situation like that?"

"Oh, I think you're getting all worked up over nothing," Paul shot back amiably. "It's all been very pleasant."

"Well, count me out anyway. I couldn't possibly take part in something I'm convinced is dangerous."

"It's up to you, Mary, but I think you're making a mountain out of a molehill," he countered. "Well, time's running short and I've got a lot more phone calls to make."

I was puzzled at the intensity of my reaction to that call. After all, Paul had years of experience with healing. It didn't make sense to be so upset. Three weeks later the mystery was solved.

Unexpected Apology

"Mary, I called to tell you I owe you an apology," Paul blurted without preamble.

"Whatever for, Paul?" I asked, "You've never done anything to offend me."

"It wasn't anything I said, but what I thought. When you refused to join the healing circle, I put it down to professional jealousy because a big time author and head of a metaphysical group was doing hypnotic regressions. Well, I was wrong and you were right. It actually happened!"

"What do you mean, 'it happened'? What happened?"

"It was just like you said," he responded, embarrassed. "A member in the group volunteered to be regressed. Next thing you know she was being burned at the stake."

"Oh, no! Who was in charge? Please don't tell me it was the high school student!"

"Nope, it was him. I've never seen anything like it."

"How dreadful! Did everything turn out all right?"

"Well, it was touch and go there for a quite a while. She was screaming in agony. Some of us jumped up and rushed over to try to comfort her. It was unbelievable! Her skin was so hot we almost burned ourselves when we touched her. It looked like she was pretty well stuck there, but finally he managed to get her back."

This was one of those times when life as an empath can be downright painful. "I can't imagine going through something like that," I gasped. "Is she okay now?"

"I can't say. She was still burning up when she left. All I know for sure is she was still having problems three days later."

"I'm so sorry for her, Paul. No one should ever have to suffer like that! In our sessions, the first thing we do is agree that there will be no pain! I wish I could help her."

"I haven't heard a thing more from her. No one from the healing circle has. I doubt if she wants anything more to do with us. But it sure taught me a lesson! I was wrong and you have my humblest apology."

"No apology necessary, Paul. I can't blame you for thinking of my work in the only context you know. Thanks for letting me know. It gives me more confidence in my own work."

"We're still friends, right?" He quipped lightly as he hung up.

Pros, Cons, and Responsibility

This evidence proved that, contrary to popular opinion, a PhD or certification in hypnosis does not qualify a practitioner to deal with real crises in other lifetimes. As valuable as hypnosis is in many other areas, this work occurs on a deeper soul level. It is not enough to command a client to go to another incarnation, monitor the session and bring them back when appropriate.

I am convinced the simple procedures we take for granted would have prevented the agony that poor woman suffered. My Spirit Guides have taught me well and fully participate in every session. It takes internal strength, compassion, and flexibility to deal with physical danger, as well as mental and emotional trials. The confidence, serenity, and intensified awareness my clients experience remind me of a favorite quote from Ray Bradbury: *"We all are rich and ignore the buried fact of accumulated wisdom."*

I believe Spirit's guidance can change any situation from a disaster into an opportunity. Years of experience taught me to stay as open and observant as possible. However, the real job is for the client: to assimilate, value, and use the gift.

"What qualifies me to serve as an instrument of Divine Purpose?" I wondered. Perhaps it's the courage, strength, and resilience of a lifetime, plus a deep spiritual belief in the inherent beneficence of the Creative Force of the Universe. The gentle power and wisdom of the Spirit who guides our journeys assures us of a successful trip and a safe return from the mysterious realm of immortal consciousness.

It's impossible to take credit for the work. However, it finally became evident that the energy I channel enables Spirit to reach us. This work has revealed many varied and surprising ways karmic issues from other lifetimes influence our responses to life challenges. It has shown by example that it's possible to heal bad karma.

Mary Blake

When I committed my life to working as an instrument of Divine Purpose I had no idea it would lead to such remarkable breakthroughs in spiritual and karmic healing. More and more I am convinced that this will be my life work.

Chapter Fourteen
Sifting the Sands of Time

On July 1st I moved into a new apartment. It was a mess. Paint stalactites hung from ceilings and closets. There was a hole in the bedroom ceiling. The kitchen was just four walls and a window—gutted to prepare for the "improvements" required to justify the rent increase. Days went by in a blur of cleaning, scraping and painting closets, installing light fixtures and lugging boxes around in a 90 to 100 degree heat wave. On July 4th two guys who didn't speak English gave the walls a thin coat of whitewash.

The job had barely begun; it would take everything I had in me to transform this long-neglected apartment into a home. Laboring non-stop through a summer of record-breaking heat waves, it didn't even register that the nausea, dizziness and weakness of heat prostration I'd suffered through my whole life were just gone. Too exhausted to even notice this blessing, l chipped away at the mountain of work.

Vanishing Phobia

Dashing out on an errand to the hardware store, I was startled to see a couple with two enormous snakes leaning against a van. I shivered involuntarily. Memories surfaced of my normally fearless child-self screaming when a schoolyard bully waved a tiny green garter snake in my face. Recollections of the terrible retching that hit me every time I came within two blocks of a snake played out behind my eyes.

My gaze shifted from the man to his snake-draped lady friend, then back to the boa constrictor he contemptuously waved at me.

"Hey lady," he taunted, "are you scared of this gentle creature? He's a very friendly snake. Touch him; I dare you!"

With surprising determination, I sauntered over and touched that huge snake. Inexplicably, the incapacitating convulsions and dry heaves didn't kick in. There was no violent reaction—none at all.

Leaving a disappointed bully behind, I strolled down the sidewalk. My casual demeanor hid overwhelming emotional turbulence and confusion. I stumbled at the curb and ducked into a nearby café to recover. Sips of iced tea gently eased the inner tumult.

The hardware store forgotten, I headed home to tackle this mystery in my own space. With candles, incense, and crystals to intensify my focus I probed for answers. Something had changed my body chemistry and eliminated a lifelong phobia. Snakes and heat... the only event that came to mind was that crazy time-trip to the dessert last winter. I sifted the sands of time swirling between 1848 and 1981 in search of a logical explanation... karma, maybe. None of the esoteric lore I'd studied provided techniques to create such weird and wonderful changes, so I began afresh.

A wave of gratitude for that belatedly recognized and acknowledged miracle welled up in me and filled the room. What would life be like now that heat and snakes were no longer the enemy? I sat pondering that thought until I realized the mystery would reveal itself in time.

Villain or Savior?

Surprisingly over the next few days I experienced twinges of guilt for a lifelong hatred of snakes. No snake had ever done anything to cause such revulsion. Yet from a block away the spoor left me heaving convulsively, dizzy, and too weak to stand. My kids knew they were on their own at the reptile house.

Bye Bye Bad Karma

The shock of touching that seven foot snake with impunity forced me to realize what a huge blessing I had received. Something inexplicable had changed my karma but I didn't know what, how much, or why. Listing the changes might help to clarify things. Here's my list:

1. After a lifetime of misery, I had just experienced no reaction whatever to two of my nemeses, a 100° heat wave and snakes.
2. Those two improbable miracles made my life immensely more bearable.
3. I'd had no psychotherapy or prescriptions to treat either of these conditions.

Last winter's virtual reality misadventure in the desert was the only lethal encounter with snakes I'd ever had. How could witnessing Mac's death by heat exposure and snakebite have erased that karma and completely eliminated my hypersensitive reactions to heat and snakes? I needed to understand how it had happened and why.

After days of meditation, questioning, and analysis, the epiphany finally came. Viewed from a different perspective, the desert drama took on an entirely new meaning. That rattlesnake was not Mac's executioner; it was his rescuer. A young, strong soldier accustomed to the rigors of war could have lain there for days suffering from starvation, sunburn, delirium, and dehydration. It would have been a prolonged, agonizing death.

Instantaneous death from snakebite saved Mac (me) from days of torture. Irrational fears engendered by his dying belief that a snake had murdered him could now be transmuted into gratitude for a mercy killing! This realization created a new harmonic resonance within my consciousness. that manifested as a profound, permanent healing. The cellular memories, and the suffering they generated, had disappeared. It made me more determined than ever to use this gift wisely.

It is clear that elimination of the original cause of karma can erase barriers to health, happiness and success. Instead of spending years in therapy, endlessly reliving events in our recent past, we can deal directly with the root cause of karmic blocks where they began, and eliminate them. What a gift Spirit has given us… me especially!!

New Challenges

In gratitude for that amazing healing, I worked even harder to serve as an instrument of Divine Purpose. I took more courses and attended lectures and seminars with leaders in many healing disciplines. Next on my bucket list was the Healing Symposium in Washington, DC. What a powerful experience!

Buckminster Fuller, a genius I had long hoped to meet, was a presenter. It turned out to be one of his last public appearances.

That was only the beginning! I had attended several of Dr. Elisabeth Kubler Ross' lectures and workshops, but had never worked with her. After lunch I noticed she was very pale and asked if she could use a bit of healing energy. She smiled and confessed she wasn't sure she could go on. We found a quiet corner where we could work. I spoke my usual silent prayer affirmation aloud for her benefit. It couldn't have felt more natural if we had been working together for years. She sank into a deep meditative state and gratefully absorbed the healing energy flooding through me. After about ten minutes she nodded to her assistant, reached for my hand and said she was ready to go on. I got an appreciative hug as she headed toward the stage. I beamed energy at her during the deeply moving, intensely personal lecture she almost hadn't given.

How rewarding to be in the right place at the right time! Later I shared a limousine ride with Dr. Virginia Satir on the way to a videotaping session of her work and mine. She was the brilliant psychotherapist whose work inspired Neuro Linguistic

Programing, an effective approach to communication, personal development and psychotherapy. My conversation with her alone was worth the trip. Despite our different paths—hers academic and mine experiential—we found that our theories were quite similar, and that our clients were experiencing results far beyond the parameters of traditional psychotherapy.

Chapter Fifteen
Accidental Encounter

At the end of the Healing Symposium I headed back to my hotel. Ruth, a fellow healer, called out to me, so I turned and waited until she caught up. Between gasps for breath, she asked if I had time for a healing. She had one of her agonizing headaches.

Despite reluctance to discuss the new therapy, my wayward mouth volunteered, "Maybe a *Soul Voyage* could help you discover the cause of your pain. I can't promise, but it might help you get rid of your migraines."

"What's a *Soul Voyage*?" she asked, "I've been working in metaphysics for years, and never heard of it."

"Look, it's hard to explain, but…" and as briefly as possible, I described the miracles happening in my life. Ruth hung on every word as if it were a lifeline.

A Gift from Heaven

"Let's do it—right now," she beamed. "This sounds like a gift straight out of Heaven."

As we walked I filled her in on what to expect. She agreed to the ground rules based on what Spirit had taught me, and what I had learned from the sessions. "While we're working, don't analyze… just let your impressions flow. Your job is to not think! Also, you must agree there will be no pain. At the slightest discomfort, we'll float your consciousness above the scene and work through whatever is going on." Within minutes we arrived at her hotel room and were on our way to a very moving adventure.

Years of meditation, metaphysical studies plus psychic gifts enabled Ruth to slip easily from deep relaxation into a state of altered consciousness. Almost instantly she was propelled into a lifetime no one would have willingly chosen.

"Can you describe your surroundings?" I asked.

The first indication of where we were came as a muffled groan. "I'm in a horrible, dark dungeon," she whispered. Her body shook involuntarily. "I'm chained to the wall, just hanging there. Oh… the rats!"

Fortunately, I was sitting on the floor, or I might have fallen off my chair. I got the impression of an emaciated, once-beautiful female agonizingly pinioned against a dank dungeon wall. How can I deal with this?" I wondered.

"I feel my life force, my body wasting away," she gasped. "I cannot stay alive much longer…"

"No! This will not do," Spirit snapped. "Remember, you agreed in advance there would be no physical pain."

I fought hard to remain calm despite the force of the command that had just burst through my lips, announcing the arrival of my rescuer.

"Float above the scene and describe it, please," Spirit directed with calm authority.

Ruth's jagged breathing slowly returned to normal. Then Spirit's usual gentle questioning began: "Who are you? Why are you here in this dungeon?"

Celantine and the Betrayer

"I'm Celantine. I'm here because it's impossible to go up against the establishment like I did, and hope to get away with it," she sighed. "But the worst pain of all is knowing that my dearest friend, my protégé, has betrayed me."

Suddenly Ruth's own voice broke through. "I know who it is!

The betrayer is my brother!"

"Back up a minute, here!" my logical mind roared in rebellion, "We don't know where she is, or what crime she has committed. We don't know anything except that she's in this dreadful dungeon. Maybe she's jumping to conclusions."

Spirit calmly responded, "Celantine, you can't come up with a workable solution with such limited knowledge. You really don't know what went wrong. This betrayer, whoever he or she was, then or now, will have to be dealt with later."

"What an exercise in futility," my left brain rattled on from somewhere above and to the left of my physical body. "What's the point of interviewing a dying person chained to a dungeon wall? It's a daunting task at best. You're out of your league," I told myself, then realized I was thinking, instead of following my own advice. "Patience," I reminded myself. "Just do your job and have faith. Spirit is in charge here."

Faith in Spirit notwithstanding, I couldn't help worrying about Ruth. This wasn't my idea of a healing! All I could do was hope against hope that years of work in a metaphysical community had equipped her for this ordeal. Slowly the conscious will surrendered and I gave up trying to second-guess Spirit. My mentor was not only game, but more than qualified for this assignment.

Interview on a Dungeon Wall

Gently, Spirit drew Celantine from the depths of hopeless agony to grudging receptivity, and finally established trust.

"Where is this dungeon?" Spirit asked.

"Um, le Midi—it's the south of France."

"Why are you in this dungeon?"

"I guess I deserved it," she murmured.

"Explain," Spirit encouraged.

"We were fighting against a satanic cult… to free the people from its cruelty and oppression. We fought so bravely to destroy their stranglehold on our people. We had such courage, such dedication… then somehow it all fell apart. How could I have failed them? Where did I go wrong?"

"Why do you choose to take the blame for this all upon yourself?" Spirit inquired.

"Because I was their leader. They counted on me." Her sense of failure was more painful by far than the torture she'd endured.

Spirit deftly deflected her pointless self-recrimination. "When did you first sense the campaign was going awry?"

"It was a feeling that came upon me… the feeling that I could no longer trust Ambrose. He was my right arm… my trusted lieutenant. He was with me from the beginning. At first I blamed myself for doubting him, but there were too many little things undone… things that left us vulnerable and my leadership in question. Suddenly he was the enemy within… a traitor… such treachery," she moaned.

In an imperious voice, Spirit cut through her woeful tale of victimization and issued clear instructions: "You can stop this before it begins! Come! I'll take you to the time, place and event which led Ambrose to betray you."

"Huh? That was a surprise," I thought. Spirit had just instructed someone on the edge of expiring to travel backwards in time to the specific event that set the stage for her incarceration and imminent demise. My first impulse would have been to go to the exact moment of betrayal. There was so much to learn!

A Calculated Seduction

The drama that unfolded left me struggling to remain silent and stay out of the action. It was a tale of high principles, heroism, and deception worthy of a Sir Walter Scott novel.

We were instantaneously transported to a shabbily furnished

room. The scene was surprisingly risqué. A voluptuous redhead was draped seductively over the young man who evidently was our target. Celantine identified the temptress as a newcomer to the group.

As we floated above the scene, silently observing, it became clear the woman was using her feminine charms to lure Ambrose into betraying Celantine… but why? As we watched, her plot to take over as leader unfolded.

"Oh, poor Ambrose," Celantine murmured softly. "He was a victim, not an enemy. Marguerite, the schemer, destroyed us both!"

"Let's go back to your headquarters," Spirit blithely suggested, "where we can resolve this matter very simply."

Done… instantly!

The group's secret headquarters were well hidden, behind and somehow beneath a nondescript inn. I got a fleeting impression of a bare table, a single candle, but as usual was only partially "there." The psychic glimpses of the drama unfolding were so fascinating it was all I could do to stay focused, keep the energy flowing and control the impulse to jump in.

Celantine's nervous energy was palpable. She paced, stomped, waved her arms about… started sentences only to abandon them half-spoken. Her frustration left her panting in helpless fury. "It's over! It was all for nothing! Everything is ruined!" she raged.

Spirit waited patiently for her to take a breath. "Nothing is irrevocable, Celantine. You can end this matter before it goes any further if you use the knowledge just gained wisely," he calmly informed her.

"What can I do? Ambrose is already in her thrall…"

"He is an innocent dupe. That woman is playing upon his vulnerability. Use this knowledge to eliminate her as an enemy."

"But how can I do that? She has very cleverly set her trap…"

"The best way is usually the simplest and most direct. Why not turn your jealous enemy into a grateful ally?"

"Mmph!" came a gasp from deep within. "Is that possible? Teach me how. If there's a way…"

"There is always a way," Spirit assured her, and proceeded to suggest ways to turn Marguerite's ambition to mutual advantage. "You could compliment her and outline a plan of your own. If it's tempting enough, she'll choose your plan and abandon her own."

"Ah," I thought, "Spirit suggested an alternative choice instead of telling her what to do. She can choose to remain bitter and tormented or take the initiative this wise being offers. The outcome… and her fate… is all up to her."

The lady listened well.

A Brilliant Strategy

"A plan. That's it! I need to make a plan," she rallied with mounting enthusiasm. "But how can I give her what she wants without stepping down and losing everything I've worked for?"

"Perhaps there's another, better way," Spirit casually suggested. "She might be much happier to be put in charge of a branch of your organization based a suitably long distance away. Of course she'd need training…"

"Oh, I see. I could offer to train her… to teach her some of the skills I've learned and help her organize her own band of defenders. It would be far less risky for her than tricking poor Ambrose into betraying me and then trying to take over my organization. Brilliant! Turn an enemy into an ally! I think it will work!"

With her quick wit, determination and strength restored, Celantine was back in command of her world. "I must send word to her and invite her here for a strategy meeting," she mused.

"Let's go forward to the moment just before Marguerite arrives for that meeting. You will have a well-drawn-out plan to offer her. She'll never suspect you are aware of her ambitious scheme of betrayal."

Bye Bye Bad Karma

I have no idea what Spirit did. Somehow the tragedy was transformed into a completely new scenario that unfolded quite naturally. Only a master strategist could have shepherded our heroine from unwary victimhood to strategic mastery.

In less than a second, there was a knock at the door. Celantine greeted her visitor enthusiastically. "Come in, Marguerite, I have something very, very important to talk over with you."

The redhead was wary, defensive, and perhaps a bit frightened, judging from the vibrations skittering past me. Celantine carried it off brilliantly. Her improvised rewrite went flawlessly. She began by praising the woman, assuring her how valuable she was and how much she was needed. Then she waxed eloquent on the importance of their cause, the tremendous effort, devotion and sacrifice demanded of their members. Next she skillfully laid the trap and offered the bait.

"Our little band cannot be everywhere at once. The enemy is on the move, Marguerite. We need strong leaders to carry our mission to other Satanic strongholds, to harry them, weaken them, and give them no rest."

My psychic impression of Marguerite's reaction was a blend of embarrassment, confusion, guilt, greed, hope and a trace of humility. I hung spellbound on every nuance.

"Oh, but Celantine, I'm not experienced enough…" she stammered. "I wouldn't know how to build a troop of loyal followers, to train them, to…"

The confident leader cut off her maudlin ramblings. "Leave that to me, Marguerite. I'll train you. I'll teach you and guide you. We'll double and treble our forces. Together we'll drive them back into their filthy holes like the rats they are!"

The redhead was on her knees, clutching the edge of Celantine's robe, pledging eternal loyalty. The candle shimmered appreciatively.

The tension in my shoulders and gut dissolved as I realized she had pulled it off. Marguerite had been neatly converted from a dangerous rival to a loyal ally. "Wouldn't Hitchcock have loved it?" I mused.

A Peaceful Departure

Spirit asked Celantine to go to her last day on Earth.

"She's old! She looks almost eighty, and round… not hugely fat, but definitely plump," Ruth chuckled.

"Thank you! Would you please describe the room? Is she alone or are there people around?"

"She's an adorable octogenarian. How could that happen? Oh, never mind! She's so peaceful and content in her own cozy bedroom. The room is full of relatives—grown children, grandchildren, so many of them… and they all love her so!"

Bypassing Ruth, the Spirit voice that wasn't really mine spoke directly to the elderly woman: "Celantine, you've lived a fine, productive, fulfilling life to be justly proud of. Understanding that this is the last day of this particular lifetime on this planet, please take a moment to tell your loved ones everything you want them to know before you leave.

The silence was so dense it felt like velvet… then a delicious, satisfied sigh filled the room. Without knowing what she said, I knew Celantine had given her loved ones exactly what they needed.

"Now that all your loved ones have your final gift to cherish," Spirit continued with impeccable timing. "You've cleared the way to leave this well-worn body behind. Once you're comfortable in your new vibrantly-alive spirit body, you can move on to the most wonderful place you are capable of experiencing."

"I'm ready," Celantine announced. "Show me how."

"Float just above your body until you're ready to leave the Earth plane behind. Take one last look at your beloved family and then we'll be on our way."

One more breath and Celantine was joyously received into the custody of her spiritual family. She… and Spirit… were no longer with us.

Ruth and I were too exhausted to do anything but fumble out of our clothes and collapse into bed. It had been an exhausting day even before we began this incredible adventure. We were asleep almost before we pulled up the covers.

Morning slid by in a blur, but we managed to catch the train back to our ordinary lives—hers in New Jersey and mine in New York City.

The trip home gave us time to review and analyze every aspect of Celantine's amazing journey. We compared impressions and memories in an effort to probe their deeper meanings. Our shared background as healers gave us a certain amount of awareness and insight, but only so much. There were so many new concepts to explore and put into their proper perspective. I had as many questions as Ruth did.

"What made you jump in and announce that the betrayer was your brother?" I blurted as we approached her stop. I couldn't wait another minute to hear her answer.

"Simple," she grinned as the train pulled into the station. "He was easily recognizable, and he's the single relative who has caused me the greatest amount of pain ever since I can remember. I was not a bit surprised that he had betrayed me in another lifetime."

She grabbed her bag and headed toward the door.

"Keep me posted," I called after her.

As she waved from the platform, I wondered what the future held for my friend. Would our medieval adventure change Ruth's future for the better as it had Celantine's? Would we even know if it did?

Pathways to Understanding

A few days after that enlightening train ride, I got my first report.

According to Ruth, changes had already begun.

"You know," she confided, "I'm already catching myself looking at things a bit differently. I have a feeling that visit with Celantine will lead to major changes in my life. Do you think the energy of that dungeon might be permanently erased from my consciousness?"

"Remember, we asked to be taken to a lifetime where events were happening that were interfering with your life today. The changes in that lifetime will be as valuable as you make them. I'd rather give my energy to the happy ending. I don't have any idea how it'll turn out, but knowing you, I can predict only positive results."

"I've got a lot of sorting to do through events in my life. It's going to be interesting to view them from a whole new perspective. I promise to keep you posted."

I could hardly wait for those reports.

"I've been examining those two lifetimes side-by-side, and have come up with some interesting theories," she announced a few weeks later. "I'm beginning to think of my brother, a.k.a. Ambrose, as a fellow victim instead of a villain."

"That's fascinating," I responded. "I got chills when you said that."

"He just might not be a total cad after all," she chuckled.

"Yeah… on this plane of imperfection there's no such thing as a perfectly bad or perfectly good person, right?"

We both laughed at that truism, then Ruth's voice took on a rueful note.

"You know, seriously, I guess I always expected the worst of my brother. What if my attitude had an effect on him, making him more rebellious than he might otherwise have been? Could the prejudicial expectations brought forward from that lifetime in France have caused me to set him up as a villain? This is a whole new ballgame! I've got to rethink everything. It never occurred to me that I could possibly have contributed to what was wrong with our relationship."

"Wow! That's a breakthrough if I've ever heard one!" I applauded.

This epiphany was the first of many. During the weeks and months that followed, Ruth used her spiritual training to move beyond the karma created in that incarnation in medieval France. The bitterness carried like old baggage through so many lifetimes gradually faded away.

One fine day I received a call describing the lovely brunch Ruth had just shared with her brother. A few days later a warm, loving note arrived. It read, "Mary, I just had to thank you for the soul trip that led to my reconciliation with Ted."

That much-appreciated recognition for a job well done convinced me that the positive changes we make in these voyages can generate unexpected rewards in our present lives.

Retracing, Refining and Reevaluating

Each dramatic trip into other lifetimes added new layers of intensity and depth to the technique. The first spontaneous regressions could have been explained away as group energy or coincidence. The solo trips with Darren, Meg and Melanie invalidated that hypothesis. The three gringos' trek through the desert added a new dimension to the trips when tragedy turned into a life-changing gift. Gratitude for that personal miracle prompted an in-depth re-evaluation of the work and hints of even greater life-changing potential.

The drama that unfolded in Ruth's hotel room raised the bar again. Spirit challenged Celantine to find a way to use newly revealed information wisely to take back her power. What a way to change karma—improvise! She turned an enemy into an asset and her whole life changed. Only a shadow of the tragedy lingered as a reminder of what can happen if we give in to negative forces.

Ruth continued to explore new possibilities that opened once that karma was eliminated. She launched new projects, gave her talents free reign and finally gained recognition as a leader in the New Jersey Metaphysical Society. Best of all, once the karmic trail of distrust was removed, she and her brother could finally enjoy a warm, loving relationship.

Word spread about my work and the positive results continued to accumulate. Evidence mounted that the expanded consciousness kindled in these journeys was permanent. I began to suspect this spiritual therapy could lead to deep, positive changes in our current lives. However, attempts to analyze the process made about as much sense as dissecting a cat to locate the source of the purr. To quote a Stalin era intellectual, "it was getting harder and harder to predict the past."

My friend Hans Holzer, a world famous paranormal researcher and author, asked, "Are you making a record of street numbers, dates on tombstones, newspaper headlines? Verifiable evidence as to location and dates would help to validate your work."

"Not really," I responded. "It just doesn't seem to matter at the time. To me, changes for the better are more meaningful than confirmation of names, dates and geographical locations." Hans was amazed at my lack of concern about validation but, always the continental gentleman, let his eyebrows eloquently express his opinion.

Each session illustrated more convincingly that these trips into other lifetimes are a gateway to a much improved version of reality. Deep emotional responses, positive changes in outlook and outcome are validation enough for me. Demographic details lack the impact of human drama. When and where we are and how we get there, I leave to Spirit.

These radically non-traditional sessions have one common thread… how real they feel. Clients assert, as if with a single voice, "It was more real than everyday life. I remember every single detail much more clearly and intensely than what happened to me yesterday… or even earlier today!"

So what is reality, I wondered. Is it what we feel as real in everyday life or something else entirely? The dictionary defines reality as:

> *"The world or the state of things as they actually exist, as opposed to an idealistic or notional idea of them.*
>
> *• a thing that is actually experienced or seen, especially when it is grim or problematic."*

More to the point, reality is always supremely subjective. What one thinks and feels during any event carries far more weight than mere "facts as they actually exist." Many of those "facts" are forgotten, overlooked or vehemently denied anyway.

I suspect the primary purpose of visiting another lifetime is to acquire knowledge and hopefully a shift in perception that will lead to a better life, ergo a better world. A minute shift in core beliefs can lead to profound life changes. New insights, awareness and understanding could well become the platform needed to create a more positive future.

Chapter Sixteen
Sharpening My Saw

A small but telling disadvantage of my unique training was a significant lack of credentials. There were no degrees or training programs for what I was doing. People who asked where I had studied had a hard time accepting that I was "Spirit taught." I asked Paul Maslow how to handle this. "You need to get certified," he insisted. Then came a vivid description of the time police raided his apartment and destroyed all his equipment. A doctor was infuriated when Paul's unorthodox treatment had healed a cancer patient he'd pronounced hopeless. In retaliation he informed the police that Paul was practicing medicine without a license.

"How can I prevent something like that from happening to me?" I asked. "The only credentials I have are from the UK. I was certified as a magnetic healer by the World Federation of Healing, and also completed three courses of study at the Society of Metaphysicians."

"That won't help," Paul assured me. "The best way is to become a nurse or a minister."

The bedpan brigade held no appeal, so that left the ministry. Paul agreed, adding that constitutional protection of religious practice would protect me, reassure clients and give credence to my work. That made sense.

I explored my options and learned the newly formed New Seminary was offering an interfaith ministry course. What a perfect way to resolve the credentials issue. I was happy to learn the founders were a "New Age rabbi," a defrocked Catholic priest, a renegade Methodist minister, and an internationally respected swami. Classes were beginning in two weeks. The whole student body consisted of 14 students. What could suit me better?

Shortly after the school year began, Meg called to tell me the book that threatened never to be finished was on the stands! At the publication party I realized her intuition was correct. Art's and Joseph's book dealing with family dynamics was hailed as a psychological landmark. Critics and experts alike predicted its remarkably astute, brilliantly presented perspective would make it required reading for psychology students. Stacks of reviews concurred.

Art didn't look well, but even if he had been open, it wasn't the time or place to voice my concern.

Credentials at Last!

In June, 1982 I graduated from the New Seminary as a Minister of Spiritual Counseling. Belt and suspenders, I was also ordained by the Spiritual Science Mother Church as Minister of Spiritual Science and joined the National Chaplain's Society for good measure. I registered at the County Clerk's Office as founder of The Church of Spiritual Discovery and hung all this evidence of legitimacy, plus the certificates earned in England, on the wall, in case the police dropped by.

The work began to gain recognition and attract prestigious clients. Harry Lipsig, a legendary New York attorney, interviewed me on his WOR public radio program. I was featured on radio stations throughout the US and Canada in interviews about regression therapy and on an NBC late night radio show. The *New York Times* holiday edition of unique gifts listed "His and Her Regressions" as the perfect Christmas gift for couples who have everything.

At the Association of Humanistic Psychology Conference in Princeton I participated in all day intensives with Carl Rogers and Marilyn Ferguson, plus workshops with Elisabeth Kubler Ross, John and Toni Lilly, Virginia Satir, George Leonard, Betty Edwards and Stanislav Grof among others. It was a weekend of inspiration, experiential learning and exposure to great minds. I returned to New York more committed than ever to explore the impact of other incarnations on current life consciousness.

That fall I received a terse message from Meg asking me to use my healing ability to help Art. I finessed my way into his hospital room with my ministerial credentials. He recognized me but the feeding tube prevented him from speaking. He wrote a couple of notes thanking me for coming. I beamed love and healing energy at him, but could do little to ease his agony.

News of his passing a few days later came as a relief. What a blessing that Art was free of agonizing pain! When I reached out to his spirit, the cosmic plan unfolded just a little. I felt his great joy at being released from the agony he'd experienced, but more than that, a huge sigh of satisfaction as he reconnected with the boy-man from Atlantis. The almost encyclopedic knowledge Art had amassed, and his brilliant intellectual achievement, had finally fulfilled the blond god's desperate hunger to learn and to use that knowledge as a force for good on this plane.

That realization taught me that Spirit was working on a level I might never fully understand. I gave thanks for the miracle that had happened and resigned myself to work with whatever was given, and do the best I could.

A Transient Gleam

More and more dimensions were being added to the work. Rest and revitalization in a cosmic retreat became a vital component at the end of each session. This multiplied the accrued benefits of the sessions and eliminated the vulnerability and disorientation often experienced by patients of hypnotic past life regressionists.

The spiritual development classes were intensifying. Amazing personal revelations and insights from Spirit became routine.

Karmic breakthroughs in private sessions proved to be anything but "trips backward in time." They were far beyond mere shortcuts to learning from "past mistakes." Each session offered at least one opportunity to deal with negative situations in a positive way and thereby eliminate karma. These sessions have taught me that suffering from bad karma is non-compulsory.

Meg's impromptu therapy session gives me chills every time I think of it. She and Spirit, working as a team, rewrote history and simultaneously changed three women's karma. The remarkable improvements in Caterina's burden of shame, Liana's new sense of self-worth, and Meg's improved health were impossible to ignore.

Spirit has since proven, in many different ways, that soul growth in one session affects many other lifetimes. It creates miraculous changes for the better in any and all other incarnations affected by the crises that were just healed. My role as passive witness to such transformative spiritual breakthroughs is enlightening, exhilarating, inspiring and, above all else, humbling. Nothing will ever be the same!

Chapter Seventeen
Al Fresco Healing

An impromptu healing happened at the Renaissance Fair, a medieval theme park in Westchester. During a stint as a "seer" a colleague asked me, as a personal favor, to work with her friend, Todd. I happened to be free right then, so agreed.

The fellow was a walking apology. I touched in with him in what started out as a routine energy healing. It was clear he had never worked with a healer. In all likelihood, this would be a tough case. The immediate arrival of Spirit confirmed that suspicion. What a relief! The spontaneous spiritual healing began with actors, horses, vendors, fairgoers as background. Gasps, mumbled responses and shivers were all Todd could manage. I felt like a paramedic administering spiritual CPR. As the healing progressed, I learned he was an astrologer but was too shy to build a practice.

As we were wrapping up, I overheard a fair visitor ask for an astrology reading. She was turned away because the concession had no astrologer. I caught her attention and told her our astrologer had just arrived and I thought I could get her an appointment. The concessionaire was delighted to have a new recruit recommended by two regulars and gave instant approval.

I pushed Todd forward and introduced him to the lady waiting for a reading. Before he could say he wasn't ready, there was a long line waiting for his services. From time to time he glanced my way seeking assurance and I'd shoot him a thumbs up. At the end of the day we exchanged cards. His said "Bass Trombone."

Back in the city, he called with profuse thanks and asked what he should do next. That was how Todd got enrolled in my spiritual development classes and a crash course in self-esteem.

He entered his first class almost stealthily, a man attempting invisibility. Hesitantly, he inquired if it was okay if he sat on the couch. Other class members noticed his discomfort and reached out to him. He was too nervous to respond to their friendly greetings. He just sat there, stiff and uncomfortable, apparently trying not to take up too much space.

After class, I suggested a private session might help him deal with his shyness. By then we had built a level of trust. Partly on faith and partly from desperation, he accepted, hoping that delving into other lifetimes might heal his tormented spirit.

Hanged Man

He lay on my couch, floating through the levels of consciousness to his safe space. Contact with his other incarnation shattered the peaceful, nourishing atmosphere. He gagged convulsively and his body thrashed about violently. Reflexively, I reached out to comfort him. Through what sounded like a death rattle, he managed a garbled plea for help. On the verge of panic, I sent out a silent plea for help. Remembering what Spirit had done in similar situations, I asked him to float above the scene and describe it. From that safe vantage point, Todd described the gallows where a public execution was in progress. His soul brother's trachea was about to be crushed by the noose.

"Oh, my God!" Todd gasped, "It's his birthday… his 21st birthday!"

Assuming we'd arrived too late, I wondered if we'd ever find out what sin he had committed.

Spirit arrived and dealt with the situation quite handily. My mouth issued instructions for Todd to float backwards to the time, place and events that had landed him on the gallows. A quick rewind took us to a scene in which he was on the verge of committing the capital offense for which he was tried and convicted.

"Can you tell me where you are?"

He mumbled an English sounding name.

"Are you near a big city?"

"Are ye stupid or summin'? Ain't y'heerd a' London?" came the cocky response in a lower class accent.

"I'm a stranger here. Can you tell me what year it is?" I asked hesitantly.

"1722," he muttered guardedly.

The poor little wretch had strong defenses. He must always have felt threatened. Thank God Spirit was in charge. It would take more patience than I had to gain his trust. I was amazed at the probing questions issuing from my mouth. Bit by bit this fellow's situation and the danger he faced was brought into focus.

A Young Tough

"What business do you here?" Spirit politely inquired.

Silence…

"We have no quarrel with you. We're here to help."

"Hah!" he spat.

"If you will tell us what's going on, we can find a way."

"An whafore an why'dja wanna bover?" he shot back.

"We've come a fair piece to help you," Spirit countered.

In the stubborn silence that followed it hit me—Spirit was speaking in vernacular!

"What you're up to's a danger more'n you know," Spirit calmly asserted. "You're better'n that."

"D'ye 'spect me to go hungry when there's food right here for the takin'? Tain't as if they's a'needin' it," he grumbled.

"And when you take it and get caught, what then?"

"Yah, I knows. They hang blokes for that, but I'm hungry; I gots nothin'. Gots to take it or else starve," he whined.

"And this isn't the first time you've poached in the landowner's woods. Hunger makes one reckless, and a rabbit fills the belly, right?"

He nodded.

"So that was it! But how had Spirit known," I wondered… ah, silly question!

Spirit proceeded to point out that stealing was not the only option. "There's other, better ways to get what you need," came the firm, logical advice.

"Name 'em!" he sneered defiantly.

A Different Game Plan

Spirit outlined a very simple approach. "Go to the landlord and ask for food."

"I hain't a beggar!"

"Of course you're not! This isn't begging. You can offer to work to pay for your supper. Or would you druther be flogged… or hanged as a thief?"

"It won't work! They don't want the likes a'me. They'll just call the sheriff, an' then I'm dog meat," he insisted.

It wasn't easy to convince this obstinate youth to try something as simple and straightforward as offering to work in exchange for food. Spirit was relentless. After much prodding and reassurance, still fearful that he might be flogged, he reluctantly presented himself at the kitchen entrance.

"The cook is coming. She's looking fierce. I told you so!" he muttered.

"Are you a craven coward then, cowed by anything bigger than a rabbit?" Spirit goaded. "Talk to her—tell her you'll work in exchange for her delicious food. Do it!"

That did it. His pride at stake, he edged toward the kitchen door and muttered at the cook: "Ma'am, ye're a cook and I'm hungry. I'm offerin' to do any honest labor to earn me some of them fine vittles," he stammered.

For a moment it seemed he was right. The cook took one look at him and rapped out her contempt.

"She sez there's no work fer the likes a'me," he whined. "Ohmigawd! It's the lord hisself—I'm in fer a floggin' fer sure!"

The lord of the manor had heard the boy's stumbling offer to work in exchange for food and was touched. "Have him cleaned up and fed, Rosie," he said kindly, "and then send him in to my study."

"Whatcher name?" Rosie demanded with obvious misgivings.

"Everbody calls me Cole," he mumbled.

"What's happening now?" I finally broke the long silence.

"She gimme a rag and tole me to go out back and clean meself. That's what's happenin'," he whispered. "I'm skeered a' what th' lord's gonna do but guess it's no worse'n dodgin' the grounds perteckers."

I held my breath through another long silence. "So what did the lord do?" I asked, unable to contain myself.

With an embarrassed chuckle he reported, "He was real perlite. Tole me this warn't no charity… that he 'spects a honest bit o' labor… a fair exchange. Whoever heerd'a a fair exchange?"

"How do you feel now?" Spirit inquired.

"Wore out. Hain't useta doin' this kinda work, but I give it me all. Guess it was good enuf. I got me supper awright, 'n a bed fer th' night b'sides."

"A warm clean bed and a full belly can bring out the best in a starving man," Spirit commented.

Time spun by magically. Spirit deftly guided him onto a new, more productive path. With a determined Spirit's encouragement, he eventually screwed up enough courage to ask if he could learn to read and do sums.

"I'm studyin' every day between workin'," he announced with pride.

Cole turned out to be an eager and gifted student. As Spirit propelled us through time, he reported receiving words of praise and rewards beyond his wildest dreams. That spurred him on to greater and greater achievements. Each step on his new path brought more confidence and status.

Was it my imagination, or was Todd growing taller? Maybe it was just that he was standing tall with pride.

Spirit guided him through an alternate lifetime that blew Todd's mind. Cole's willingness to learn and serve his mentor won him a special place in his benefactor's heart. His face reflected the change in status, as did his grammar and pronunciation.

"M'lord says I'm so good at my sums he's going to let me do the books. Now I don't have many outside chores. What a fine life I have," he crowed.

"We're going forward to a time when something very important is happening," Spirit intoned.

Cole collapsed, sobbing uncontrollably.

"What's causing you so much pain?" Spirit gently inquired.

"It's m'lord. His heart gave out."

Cole's grief at the lord's passing was immense.

"Not that it matters much, but I suppose all this had to end sometime," he sighed. "Guess it's time to move on."

"Wait! Offer condolences and do whatever you can to comfort the others in their grief. You're needed here," Spirit declared.

Despite his own overwhelming grief, Cole did just that. Then, in shock, he sputtered, "No! I can't believe it! How could that be?"

The bulk of the childless lord's estate had been willed to him. It was a considerable fortune. The newly acquired wealth was thrilling, but Spirit was not finished with Cole. "Take us to the next important thing that happens," he encouraged.

"I'm bored," came the apathetic reply.

"What can be so depressing? Seems you have everything a man could want," Spirit commented.

"Hmm," came his thoughtful reply, "this life of leisure isn't all that appealing after a while. All I'm doing is loafing around.

Drinking and gambling is not nearly as exciting as you might think, but there's not much else to do."

In my little bubble, I sadly pondered the situation. It didn't seem logical that Cole had been rescued from the gallows only to live a life of boredom and decadence.

Payback Time

"Remember how poor, how ragged and hungry you were when you first came here?" Spirit reminded. "Think about how grateful you were for the chance to learn. Why don't you look around and see if you can find a local boy who is as needy as you used to be. Maybe you could teach him a few things… the way your benefactor taught you."

"I can do better than that! I can build a school and teach many boys. I have plenty of money and all the time in the world. Why not? It'll be fun! I'll call it 'The Nicolby School,' after my own real name."

We skipped through time as Cole threw himself eagerly into the project. Once he had chosen a positive, constructive path, Spirit sent him forward in time once again to the next important event in his life.

"Where are you now? What's happening?" I asked, making a conscious effort to rein in my imagination.

The response came through in a mature voice laden with confidence. "I'm receiving an award from the city fathers for my role in building and funding the finest school in our shire." he answered. "Our boys have made me very proud."

After this well-earned recognition of achievement, Spirit asked Cole to go to the final day of the rewarding life he was now living.

"Please describe where you are," Spirit asked.

"I'm in my own bedroom. Everyone's here—the doctor, my servants, graduates from my school, the mayor… they're so sad!"

"What year is it?" I blurted, mindful of Hans's urging.

"It's December in the year of our Lord 1743."

"1743? How can this be? Even Spirit…" my thoughts ricocheted between those two disparate death scenes. The drama was moving so fast I could barely keep up. "Okay, re-focus, there's no time to indulge in philosophy here," I reminded myself.

"You have lived a rewarding life as a patriarch and philanthropist," Spirit glibly summed up. "You contributed greatly to many lives and to your community. Now take a look at Todd, your soul brother's life. He needs a friend like you to help him find his own path to greatness. Would you be willing to work with him as a spirit guide?"

"I would be more than delighted to work with Todd as a spirit guide," Cole assured us. "He has much to give to your world. His talents have so far been buried in self-doubt."

"That would be wonderful but I don't know how," Todd interjected.

"You can choose a word or a phrase to use when you want to contact each other," Spirit suggested.

How simple! Within a few minutes Todd and Cole had chosen signals to facilitate future communications and said farewell for now. Spirit brought a rejuvenated Todd back to New York City and "normal consciousness," whatever that might be.

Todd stretched, opened his eyes and hugged me fiercely.

"I can't thank you enough," he sang. "See you in class." With a smile that wouldn't quit, he almost danced out the door.

I collapsed onto the nearest chair and gave thanks for the miracle that had just happened. I was there… and did a miracle ever happen! Did I imagine it or was his voice deeper?

Change Upon Change

Todd burst into the next week's class, greeted everyone cheerfully and casually announced, "I think I'll sit here."

Class members glanced at each other in confusion. "Is this the same guy?" a student whispered to me.

"Tell you later," I winked.

During the next few weeks, the thoroughly inhibited young man who had tiptoed into class on a walking apology blossomed. He was buoyant, confident, and enthusiastic. His social life improved; he joined a chorus and got a better job.

Todd's amazing transformation after Spirit had helped Cole change his karma sparked lively discussions in class. "How could that be?" they wondered. All he could say was, "All I know is that when Cole's hard work changed his future, it changed mine, too. You can't imagine how real it was… you just had to be there."

Silently I echoed that thought as I charged the crystals and touched in with each one to harmonize and synchronize the class energy. We dedicated the class to the greatest good and as our voices blended in the beginning prayer-mantra, I floated away.

It was dark when I returned to so-called normal awareness at the end of the Spirit Dialogue. The whole room buzzed with excitement. Our Indian astrologer, blessed with total recall, filled me in, as usual. After complimenting individuals and the group progress, Stardust, my Number One Spirit Guide, began with a mini lecture, and then introduced a very special Spirit guest. Not surprisingly, the hot topic of the evening was consciousness, its many aspects and levels. Finally, someone asked how changes made in other lifetimes could affect us here and now. Here is Spirit's answer:

> *"When you change a recurring reaction pattern you change everything! The changes you, Spirit, and your other incarnations make are registered and stored the same way as everything that happens in your so-called 'normal daily life'… in the core consciousness. That's the evolving, ever expanding, eternal part of you… your immortal human spirit."*

Mary Blake

Reality or Illusion

Todd was not the only one changed by Cole's dramatically improved life. I was there too, hearing Spirit's words as they came through me and feeling with Todd. Each time Spirit raised the bar it led to more intimate and meaningful interactions between incarnations that produced remarkable results. Both Celantine and Cole took the initiative when Spirit offered the opportunity, made plans and carried them through on their own. Then, stretching the bounds of credibility, their positive choices and actions led to longer, happier, more fulfilled lives. Hours of research in books and articles on the subject yielded no clue as to how this could happen.

I've often thought about the choices we make that change our lives for the better or the worse. Most of us have spent a bunch of wasted time on "what ifs." That's an easy way to get mired in illusion. My work with Spirit gives me hope that we just might not be stuck forever with our wrong choices. Wouldn't it be great if we could keep the lessons and trash the pain, the resentment, the lost time, the wasted potential that we cheated ourselves out of by making that fateful decision?

During a lively class discussion sparked by the 18th century adventure Todd shared with us someone asked, "How can simply improvising a positive experience on a consciousness level change anything?" I pointed out that Spirit had calmed Lorna's fear of dying by assuring her everything was happening on a consciousness level. That shift in consciousness changed her life.

According to the experts, any changes in the past would cause disastrous results. When skeptics insisted that changing events from the past was just an illusion, I had no ready answer.

Stardust popped in to settle the confusion. As usual, her explanation was clear, concise and comprehensive:

Bye Bye Bad Karma

"Nothing that has ever happened to anyone, anywhere, any time is important. The only thing that matters is how it affects the consciousness."

Chapter Eighteen
Girl With Lives and Lives and Lives

The telephone wires crackled with an overload of distress signals. The caller rambled disconnectedly, inquiring along the way as to my experience with past life regressions. It seemed as if it all was some bird's fault. I did my best to reassure her as to my experience and capability. She chattered on about how horribly embarrassed and ashamed she was that she hadn't called me sooner.

Nothing she said made any sense… especially the part about the bird. I suggested she slow down and start from the beginning. Taking a deep breath, she started afresh. The bird turned out to be her English girlfriend, who was fascinated with past life regressions. During a visit to New York, Birdie had waxed on enthusiastically about the subject. To Ricky, an aspiring actress, it seemed like a romantic play. She was intrigued. Well into a bottle of wine and wee-morning-hours girl talk, they played with the idea of doing separate regressions and comparing notes. On a wave of enthusiasm they made a pact to do that, each on their own side of the Atlantic.

"Birdie," she continued, "dived right in as soon as she returned to England. She called and told me every thrilling detail of her regression experience. Then she asked, 'And how was yours? I can't wait to hear about your past lives.'

"I was ashamed to confess I hadn't gotten up the courage to do it," she admitted, "so I told her it was hard to find a reliable regressionist in New York. All this time I've just been hanging back, wavering between fascination and fear of the unknown. I tell myself it's much easier for Birdie because in her country there are spiritualists all over the place. She's already visited a bunch of them. You can't imagine how embarrassing it is when she tells me all about her latest adventure in some other lifetime. Then she asks when I'm going to do it and I feel like crawling under a rug."

"Got the picture. So how did you find me?" I asked.

"Well, after about a year, I finally ran out of excuses. I asked Birdie to help me find someone. I also asked all my friends in New York if they knew any local regressionists. I made a list of everyone they recommended and sent it to Birdie for her approval. She wrote back and said Mary Blake was the only name on the list that got the spiritual go-ahead. So here I am. I finally got the nerve to call you."

"When would you like to come for a session?" I sighed.

"Well, could I just come for an interview… uh… to see if I'd be comfortable working with you?"

"If that's what you want, I can set aside a few minutes to see you. When?"

"Well, I don't know…"

"Are you sure you want to do this, Ricky?" I broke through her hesitation, "Or would you rather just go on procrastinating? It's up to you. I'm running out of time here."

A Tenuous Commitment

Hesitantly she set an appointment to meet to see if she felt she could work with me.

Ricky was forty-five minutes late for the courtesy interview she had requested. The man scheduled for the next appointment was already deep into another reality when the bell rang signaling her tardy arrival.

I debated whether to answer the downstairs bell or not. Then I heard myself asking Ed to wait in a lovely garden, relax and commune with his spirit guides while I spoke with Ricky.

Bye Bye Bad Karma

Wondering what Spirit had in mind, I buzzed her in. With that small window of time freed up, I had a few minutes for a brief meeting. Hopefully I could manage to ease her concerns and let her know she was in the right place, but at the wrong time.

"Sorry, Ricky," I whispered as I greeted her at the door. "I can't see you now. I only had a half hour between appointments. There's a gentleman on my couch who needs my total attention."

"Oh, I'm sorry," she mumbled. "I didn't realize it would matter if I got here a little bit late."

"I'm not sure what you want of me," I said as patiently as possible, "but please make it quick. I can't leave that poor man stranded in another lifetime all by himself for very long."

My appearance and professional manner apparently reassured her. We made an appointment for a session the following week.

"Please do your best to be on time," I whispered, "so you won't interrupt another session."

Without further thought, I quickly returned to the journey in progress. My client's relaxing time in the garden had turned out to be quite beneficial. We were able to go much deeper into his other lifetime than I had hoped.

"Sorry about the interruption," I commented as I wrapped up the session. "I hope I didn't disturb you."

"What interruption? Oh, you mean when you took me to that beautiful garden? I thought that was part of the trip. Revelling gave me a chance to get used to being somewhere else."

We both laughed and the happy voyager was on his way. Thankfully, Ricky's energy had neither rattled the client nor disrupted the session. It turned out to be a remarkable, extremely insightful experience for him

Once again I gave thanks for the miracle that had just happened. It seemed they were showing up quite regularly.

Mary Blake

A Tentative First Voyage

Ricky arrived on time for her obligatory (and presumably only) "regression." Despite assurances from both sides of the Atlantic, she was still nervous and apprehensive. I suspected this gorgeous, statuesque young woman had grandiose expectations. She must have indulged in more than a few fantasies in anticipation of this moment. Was she anticipating an encounter with la Duse, Bernhardt… or perhaps Marie Antoinette?

It took quite a bit of patient reassurance, several relaxation techniques and guided imagery to enable her to enter the altered state necessary to proceed into another lifetime. The biggest challenge was getting past her assumptions. Agonizing moments passed by with nothing but an occasional sigh or grunt.

"Can you describe what you see?" I prompted, praying that Spirit would take over.

"All I see is black…"

Spirit finally arrived and with unfathomable patience, stuck with her until she eventually broke through the dense blackness to a dim awareness of light.

"Can you tell us where you are, please?"

"Same place's always. Wiedyawannaknaow?" Gone were the well-rounded vowels of the aspiring actress.

"Whew!" I thought. "Finally!"

"We come as friends," Spirit assured her. "We're here to help you in any way we can."

As usual, I was the last to know who she was or where we were. It felt like a verbal tug-o-war. Attempts to draw her forth, offers of friendship and helpfulness were met with silent hostility or a grudging "humph." The accent sounded almost, but not quite, cockney. My busy left hemisphere searched for an opening of any kind that Spirit could use, maybe a simple question that didn't require a commitment.

"Tell me, what are you wearing," Spirit prompted.

"Me only dress 'cept for m'church goin's… not that it's often I kin go."

"My name is Mary." I volunteered, hoping she would be more comfortable with a female. "What's yours?"

"Rachel."

After that small victory came another wall of silence. Drawing information from her was like walking knee deep in mud. Every syllable was spat forth grudgingly.

"Tell me about the room you're in, Rachel," Spirit smoothly inquired.

"I'm in the lie-berry, a`course… dustin' th' books like always."

"Do you like books, Rachel?'

"Nah, can't read. What good are they? They jist collect dust."

"Is this your home?"

"Nah, I just lives here. It b'longs to Mr. Townsend. He's rich, an' very p'tikelyar about his books'n his pretties… 'n him so old 'n ugly 'n mean 'n all!"

"Do you work for Mr. Townsend?"

"Humph! Slavin's more like it! So many rooms to clean, 'n all of 'em full a' stuff he don't deserve," she growled.

"Is Mrs. Townsend kind, at least?"

"She's long dead, poor thing. Prob'ly kilt her just livn' wif him!"

"Why do you stay here if you're so miserable?"

"Can't go nowhere till me term is up'n 'at won't be fer years," she sighed.

Bound To Service

"I'm not sure what you mean by 'term,'" I asked, unable to hold myself back at this point. "I'm from far away and everything's so different where I come from."

"Far from home, y'say? I knows all about that. But things was very bad back home," she sighed. "An' seein' as I was too plain to marry, I got sold off 'n shipped over here to this 'New World.' They call it 'denture but I calls it slave'ry."

How ironic! Ricky had expected to land in a luxurious, glamorous life. There was no room for illusion here. I wondered how she was handling this disappointment. Pity for both of them welled up in me. No wonder it was so hard to get anything but monosyllables from Rachel. She hated her life. "What are we doing here?" I wondered. "How can anything positive come from such a miserable situation?"

"What gives you joy?" Spirit asked in a kind, gentle tone. "Tell me about your hopes, your dreams."

"There he is, back by the horse run. The love a' me life."

"Who is he? Does he live here too?"

"He lives out in the stable with the horses. He's very strong. He's real smart, too. He knows all about horses… how to train 'em, wash 'em down, shoe 'em, 'n fix the bridles 'n saddles. He's the handsomest man I ever seen. Late at night I sneak out to… to be wif Rak."

Satisfied he'd learned enough, Spirit asked her to go to the next important event in her life.

Tragedy!

Ricky's body arched in pain-filled paroxysm. Rachel sobbed, "He's dead, he's dead… and I might as well be dead too!"

"What happened, Rachel?" I blurted, empathizing with her pain.

"It was in the stables. That mean horse he was working with bolted. His hoof smashed right into Rak's head 'n' now he's gone. Dead and gone forever," she sobbed.

In my little bubble, my heart ached for her. "That poor girl! Now she has nothing, I'm afraid."

Spirit, unperturbed, urged Rachel to go forward in time once again, to the next stage of her life.

"Where are you now, Rachel?" came Spirit's patient questioning.

"In the library, dusting the books." The accent was less cockney and more American, but the voice was still laden with bitterness.

"When will your term be over?"

"Oh, that's long past. When me term was up Mr. Townsend offered me the chance to stay on as his wife. Wife, humph!" she added sotto voce, "more like a permanent servant."

"How sad to wind up the reluctant wife of a crotchety, demanding old man," I thought to myself. "What a drab, loveless existence. Sounds like we've reached the point of no return."

Spirit knew better. "Rachel, I'd like to formally introduce you to your soul sister, Ricky. She really needs your strength, your common sense and your patient endurance. You can help her in many ways… perhaps even help her to appreciate her own beauty and grace, the good things she has."

"I notice she's never married, though she's headin' towards thirty," Rachel observed. "Humph! Well, she's lucky she has dreams.

Might as well stick around and peek in whenever I can and keep remindin' her to appreciate what she's got."

In my little bubble, I was delighted at the victory for both of them. Rachel beamed with pride, having something special to give. Ricky could look forward to insights from a spirit guide honed by hardship into an iron will to survive. "What a pair they'll be," I chuckled to myself.

Spirit instructed the two of them to choose signals that would make it easy to reach out to each other. Ricky's "Got it!" clinched the deal. That settled, Rachel was escorted to her well-deserved spiritual reward.

Ricky jumped at the chance to go to an ideal place to recover from her ordeal. She was whisked off to a virtual spa somewhere in the space-time-spirit continuum for much-needed rest and recuperation.

Summing Up

A few minutes later Ricky sat up and echoed my amazement at the lifetime she'd just visited. "That was the last place in the world I could ever imagine being," she gasped. "What could I possibly have in common with that poor woman? It proves it's real, I guess. To tell the truth, once I took the plunge I was sure I'd land in exotic surroundings. I was positive I was an important person… possibly a queen or a famous actress."

I nodded sympathetically, not quite sure how to respond. She sat silent for a moment, lost in contemplation.

"Tell you one thing," she confided, 'I've got a vivid imagination, but there's no way I could have come up with a scenario anywhere near that. How degrading!"

"All I can say is that Spirit is always right on target." I offered. "You've just been given unexpected gifts."

"What do you mean?" she demanded.

"Consider all the advantages of life you enjoy… the tremendous opportunities you have compared to Rachel's limited world. You have so much to be truly grateful for," I smiled. "You were just offered an opportunity to rethink your life and count your blessings. Think about Rachel… how little she had, how ignorant, poor and miserable she was. The disparity between her life and yours will surely give you a greater appreciation of your beauty, your talent… the freedom you enjoy, and the way you live. And don't forget, you now have a very down-to-earth spirit friend to help keep you on track."

"I would never have thought of it that way. All I could think about was how relieved I am to finally have something to report to my friend in England. Wait till Birdie hears about this!" she crowed.

"I'm so glad you're pleased," I responded.

"According to Birdie," she announced, "her sources think I need a bunch of these sessions. I have no idea how many Birdie's had already. Now that I've found someone I can trust, I guess we'd better set up a schedule. Can I get a discount for ten sessions?"

"Okay," I laughed, "let's sit down and agree upon a reduced rate… we'll call it a quantity discount."

More Questions Than Answers

After Ricky left I spent quite some time wrestling with the questions her session and her comments had brought up. I wondered who Birdie's sources might be. Perhaps someone I'd met at SAGB, or the Mind Body Spirit Festival or a workshop remembered me. That reminded me of the well-respected psychic who predicted I'd create a new, powerful healing technique. Perhaps she had received some new information. I wondered if this work was what she had meant. Hmm… there were so many unknowns to puzzle through.

Ten separate sessions with one client was something new.

I wondered if it had been wise to agree to the arrangement. So far I felt she'd received amazing benefits from one session. What might we expect from ten… phenomenal, or repetitive and boring results?

There was so much more to learn. The possibilities seemed endless. No matter how tortured, dreary or miserable, the lives we visited were replete with positive benefits. From my perch in the catbird seat, nothing was a total loss, no matter how negative it seemed. Expectations denied were replaced by far more valuable truths. Every time I thought I knew what was going on, more mysteries surfaced. This work was turning into one amazing revelation after another.

Chapter Nineteen
Toonshi

The next session with Ricky was dramatically different. Confident and at ease, she slipped into altered consciousness easily. We landed lightly in a dense forest. With spirit guidance, Ricky spiraled down into a heavily wooded area and located her alternate incarnation, a strapping, handsome young American Indian.

"What may I call you?" Spirit inquired.

"Toonshi," came the laconic reply.

"Could you tell us where we are?" asked Spirit.

"In the forest."

"Can you tell us where the forest is located?" Spirit prompted.

"It's just the forest. It's home." Toonshi stated flatly.

"We come from far away, from a very different time," Spirit patiently explained. "Your soul sister, Ricky, is here to visit with you. Can you touch in with her and see if you can learn what she calls the forest where you live?"

Spirit's casual request jarred me into full attention. How would a native North American react to 20th century names for "his" home?

"Humph... crazy name," Toonshi grunted. "She calls it New Hampshire. How can forest be new? Is so old—been here always."

"Ricky's people want to make up names for places. It makes them feel better." Spirit adroitly changed the subject. "Can you tell us what your people call themselves?"

"We are Chickewah," he announced proudly.

"What are you doing, Toonshi?"

"Making canoe from big tree. It is very fine canoe. Make me

very proud. Take me far… across lake, down river… where I want to go. Is good to have big canoe like this to hunt, fish, bring home game."

Them

"Do you ever see white men around here?" Spirit asked casually.

"Hah! Them," he spat. "A small number showed up a few moons ago. How can you say they men?" he remarked contemptuously. "They so fearful they make small, smelly wood caves, clutter up with things no one want and lock themselves inside!"

"That must seem very strange to one so accustomed to freedom," Spirit commented. That elicited an appreciative grunt.

Toonshi continued his acute observation of this strange new breed. "White man think they can own land. No one can own land. Belongs to Great Father. But they take much more than land. They steal peace, upset tribe, destroy our world. They offer worthless things in exchange for our heritage." His tone revealed a deep abiding sadness at this unfairness.

"Ricky's preoccupation with possessions, fame and fortune must be undergoing some kind of reassessment," I speculated.

We took Toonshi forward in time. Revelling in his new freedom, he paddled downriver, explored the white man's settlements and learned their language. Then he used his canoe to deliver pelts and freshly-caught fish to the settlers. Profits from trading financed further adventures. Toonshi was becoming quite the entrepreneur.

Though he often encountered and dealt with the "invaders" as he called them, his respect and loyalty lay with his own people… his own superior way of life.

"The more I see the less I like," he'd comment after describing with improved English how difficult it was to deal with the settlers' strange habits and foolish notions. "They don't have the skills and wisdom to live at peace with the forest. I have what they need. Yet they argue, they haggle, they cheat. They don't want to pay fair price. It not manly. Why it so hard to be honest… pay fair price?"

His intelligence and curiosity took him further and further away from his home turf.

One more leap forward took Toonshi to his last day on Earth. One evening he was shot by a fear-driven shop owner who mistook him for a savage come to burn and pillage his possessions.

Spirit easily assisted Toonshi into his new spirit life. "Open yourself to the new power and knowledge now available to you."

An eloquent "Aaah!" was all he could muster.

"Toonshi," Spirit continued, "you're only beginning to realize the vast freedom, knowledge and potential awaiting you. There are many choices ahead. If you choose you may work with Ricky as a spirit guide. She was there for you through the rough patches. Now you can help her."

"Speak to her as the ancestors spoke to me when I was a child?" Toonshi asked. "But she is white woman. How can this be done?"

Spirit patiently assured him it could be easily done since Ricky was his soul sister. Toonshi proudly accepted the chance to work as a spirit guide and help this strange white woman appreciate his values. Spirit instructed them how to set up recognition signals. Then Toonshi was off to claim his new energy body, eager as ever to explore and master all there was to learn.

Ricky was escorted to a custom-made cosmic spa to be refreshed and invigorated after her ordeal. She would need it to face the high octane energy of New York City.

Ricky emerged from that session a very changed young lady. She sat speechless, staring into space. I offered her tea, which she gratefully accepted.

"Oh, my," she gulped. "That was more than I bargained for. That Indian was so handsome, so virile…" She stopped short, out of ways to describe the emotional residue she was grappling with.

The tea worked its restorative magic. I could swear Ricky

seemed more grounded, more in touch with her surroundings than she had been a couple of hours ago.

"Now you have something interesting to report," I reminded her. Birdie will be fascinated to hear about this, I'm sure."

Ricky slipped into her coat and, half out the door, turned back. "I almost forgot," she purred… "now I have two spirit guides. I can't lose!"

Chipping Away

In counseling, Ricky and I worked together to turn clues gleaned in her sessions into usable information. We analyzed each of the plots and characters to discover their significance in the karma affecting her current life. We both felt we were chipping away at minor obstacles to clear the way to deal with a major issue head on. It was like peeling an onion, layer by layer.

Each session added new clues to the "big picture." We visited a priest in Barcelona who gratefully acted upon information revealed by Spirit that resolved issues impinging upon Ricky's life.

 The puzzling ambivalence to her Catholic upbringing made more sense when we probed the residue of energy from that lifetime. Spirit revealed the torment the priest had endured before he was offered a way to choose a happier and more productive life. She was thrilled at his choices and relieved to finally to be free of resentment of her family's religious devotion.

In another session we watched helplessly as a clumsy, good-natured farm laborer with dreams of conquering the "godless infidels" stubbornly ignored Spirit's advice. He set off to the Crusades, overburdened with weapons and armor. To Ricky's dismay, the poor guy was trampled to death by his own comrades in arms… asphyxiated in the mud before even leaving European soil.

Ricky was ready to classify it as a waste until we talked it through in a counseling session. Finally she got the message it held for her. "Oh, if he'd only listened... poor guy!" she sighed. "But y'know, there have been a few too many times when things would have gone better for me if I'd just listened. Gotta remember that one and count it as a gift," she smiled. For that she got an extra hug. Halfway down the hall she turned with a grin: "I think I'll talk this over with my spirit guides."

Monitoring Progress

That was what I call progress. The real value of our work hinged upon Ricky's willingness to work through her habitual reaction patterns and move forward. In phone conversations and counseling sessions she alternated between bouts of denial and flashes of truth, her concept of reality in a state of flux. It was quite a challenge for her to deal with other lifetimes and their surprising impacts upon her present life.

Ricky had grown up with a sense of not quite belonging in her large Catholic family. One sister had lived in New York for several years but they only spoke at family gatherings in Boston. "Come to think of it," she commented, "I don't seem to have anything in common with anyone in my family."

"As far as I can tell," I ventured, "progression of the soul from one incarnation to another has very little to do with genealogy. You might enjoy our spiritual development classes. As a member of the group, you could communicate with different spirits, soak up the energy and meet some really nice people." She leapt at that suggestion and soon became a regular.

This was a very complicated human being with many layers to unravel. In the classes and our bi-monthly trips into other lifetimes, Ricky and Spirit explored the minor issues to be resolved before we could get to the deeper causative events. We analyzed minor triumphs, assuming we'd eventually get to the belief system that was keping her in that unsatisfying loop. Each session presented totally new and different challenges.

With growing confidence in the process, Ricky knew each session moved her a step closer to a definitive combination of cause and effect. She resolved to keep digging and chipping away until the pieces would finally fit together.

For my part, I felt privileged to have the rare opportunity to witness her progress in so many forays into multiple incarnations. Most clients were thrilled with the revelations uncovered in one lifetime. I might never see them again because it never occurred to them that additional visits could multiply the benefits. I knew for sure that elimination of karma from one other incarnation could make a dramatic improvement in current reality.

Evolving Concepts

The body of evidence kept accumulating. It didn't matter who arrived at my door to venture forth into other lifetimes, or how divergent their backgrounds. Despite differences in education, culture, worldliness, curiosity, or deep-felt need, each one of them walked out changed in some unique way.

Once clients returned to the "real world," the ball was in their court. What they did with the knowledge, their willingness and determination to work with what they had learned, would determine the final outcome. The changes were often unexpected and remarkable. Some experienced transparently obvious, radical clearing right away. Others, relieved of karma they didn't know they had, were slower to acknowledge the subtle changes that gradually occurred. How deeply, how powerfully, and in what ways their lives would be affected was as varied and unique as the individuals themselves.

Most reports were glowing. To some, the gift was too private and personal to discuss. In that case I had to respect their privacy and settle for their sincere, deeply felt gratitude as they disappeared from my life.

There was no getting used to the phenomenon because, just as no two people are identical, no two sessions were alike. There was none of the weary acceptance or boredom that one often feels about an oft-repeated task. I just plainly couldn't get enough of it. The endless variety of lifestyle, locale, timeline, awareness and receptivity of the disparate incarnations we tapped into was intriguing.

I continued attending classes, seminars and workshops to acquire more professional expertise. However, without question I was learning far more from Spirit. I began to look forward to each session as another opportunity to study with a master.

No empath could witness, listen to, and communicate with people experiencing such life-changing events without being changed in many unexpected ways. It took more patience, humility, and depth of understanding of the human condition than I thought myself capable of. Though unable to take credit for the miracles, I finally acknowledged the value of my role as facilitator and energy source.

Somewhere along the way words like *always*, *never*, and *reality* became meaningless. The cumulative evidence of the limitless, ever-expanding potential of consciousness (the immortal human soul) was changing everything.

Chapter Twenty
What If Everything Goes Wrong?

A young man from class shyly asked if I had special rates for students. Knowing his part-time job left little for indulgences, I cut my student fee in half and secured his promise not to tell anyone what he was paying for his session.

Josh arrived promptly. After the obligatory orientation and relaxation techniques, he was dumped into one of the most depressing lifetimes I could ever have imagined. He was immediately drawn to a middle-aged male.

"Could you describe this person?" I asked.

"It's hard to tell what he looks like," Josh responded thoughtfully. "He's covered from head to the soles of his feet with dirt. But it's not like garbage or filth. It's the soil… earth. Instead of shoes he's got rags tied with bits of leather on his feet."

"This has to be the Dark Ages," I thought.

This was way beyond my skill level. Reflexively, I sent out an urgent SOS to Spirit.

"What may I call you?" I asked, stalling for time.

"Neb."

"Where are you?"

"In the field," mumbled the gravelly voice.

Between the Furrows

"What are you doing?" the kindly voice of Spirit inquired. "Thank you, God!" I beamed with silent gratitude and relief. Until my rescuer arrived, I hadn't realized how tense my body had been.

"Plowing," the muffled answer came through the figure on my couch.

"I see neither horse nor ox," Spirit commented.

"Ox died."

"And now you pull the plow by hand?"

"Hafta."

"It must be a terrible strain on you," Spirit commented.

"Ya gets useta it."

"Are you married?"

"In better days… she died."

"How sad for you."

A racking sigh tore through him. I reeled with shock at the dreadful life unfolding before me.

"How about children?" Spirit prompted.

"They was taken… boy and girl both… slavers y'know."

"Slavers?"

A startled "Huh?" popped out of me. It hadn't occurred to me that there would be white slave traffic in a rural area in Europe.

"That's what I call 'em," he explained. "They takes young'uns to serve out their lives slaving in some manse or worse… dunno where."

"Have you tried to find them?" Spirit asked.

"Walked me feet off searching long into the night, callin' 'em by name till I lost me voice. I talks like this ever since."

"Let's go forward in time a few years," Spirit suggested. "Tell me where you are now."

"At the end of the row, draggin' the plow around to head back into the next furrow."

I shuddered. "This is too much for a man to bear," I thought, and steeled myself for an eventual tongue lashing.

"Go forward a few more years," Spirit urged, "and tell me what's happening."

"Can't make it to the end of the row. Back's gone out again."

"Let's go to the end of this lifetime… your last day on this Earth. What's happening?"

"A beggar came along an' I giv 'im my plow. Twarn't no use t'me no more.

"That was very generous of you."

"He give me a cup'a gruel. Nice 'n hot…"

"It's time to move on now, Neb," Spirit announced with a degree of compassion I'd rarely heard. "You don't have to suffer any longer. I'm going to take you to the most wonderful place you could ever imagine. All your pain and loss will vanish and dwindle into a memory. Your loved ones. your wife and children and more… are there waiting for you."

"If you're talkin' 'bout Heaven, they won't want the likes'a me," he mumbled.

"You're so wrong Neb."

"What's a dirt grubber got t'do to get inta Heaven?"

"You've already done more than enough. Willingly you suffered for imaginary sins committed in far off lands by soul brothers you can't even remember."

A Hint of Avarice

I got a psychic flash of a hugely overweight, be-jeweled miser with cruel eyes counting a pile of coins and precious stones. "Ugh!" I winced, "that self-indulgent incarnation must be the origin of the karma that led to Neb's dreadful life." I suspected Neb had glimpsed it too. I hoped he grasped the significance of a prior lifetime that had been driven by gluttony and avarice.

His next comment, "Never understood folks that lust for more'n they need," confirmed that he fully understood.

"Your suffering was not for naught, Neb," Spirit continued. Your patience and endurance of hardship has transformed your soul from a willful, spoiled hedonist to a courageous man willing to give his only possession to a stranger."

"Never thought nothin' about it. T'warn't nothin'," Neb grunted.

"Come with me, Neb, I'll lift you far above all this weariness, pain and loss."

Suddenly the sadness that had been building in me while Neb's story unfolded melted away. "Spirit's voice alone could heal any soul, no matter how troubled," I mused.

Neb's huge jagged sigh held more emotion than I could have imagined Josh could bear.

Spirit gently lifted Neb's spirit and floated him away from that broken body. I could feel his spirit releasing the weight of an immeasurably painful lifetime and lightening in the first phase of soul expansion. Josh's face reflected confusion, wonder, and finally the most peaceful contentment I had ever witnessed.

Now came the transition back to what we think of as normal consciousness. During the rejuvenation time Josh so desperately needed, I fairly shook, dreading what would probably happen when the student I knew returned. How would he deal with all this tragedy? I wouldn't blame him one bit if he was furious. No matter what he had expected, it couldn't have been anything like this!

How Profound

Once his consciousness returned to his body, Josh stretched, opened his eyes and, to my astonishment, smiled.

In a soft, awe-filled voice he solemnly announced, "That was the most profound experience of my entire life!"

I barely managed to choke back an apology as I assured him how glad I was he felt that way. He would never know the strain I had endured during our time with Neb.

Josh gathered his things and readied himself to re-enter the "real world." I did my best to reinforce whatever Spirit and he had accomplished during that encounter with life in the Dark Ages. I fervently hoped he'd sort it out and come through it stronger. Our parting hug seemed especially meaningful to him. I couldn't ever remember his joining in individual or group hugs during or after class. He promised to call if he had questions, or just wanted to talk; then he turned and silently slipped away.

As soon as the door closed I collapsed, sending up paeans of praise and gratitude to Spirit for once again bailing me out. Alone with my thoughts, I felt strangely unsettled. Was anything resolved, really? The happy ending I had come to expect hadn't happened this time. For the first time since the beginning of this work, I felt lost, uncertain and incompetent. I couldn't shake the unsatisfied feeling.

My thoughts kept bouncing back to the "previous life of excess" Spirit had allowed us to see. I wondered why Spirit hadn't taken Neb to that lifetime and worked through those issues. I suspected tons of bad karma had been racked up in that one lifetime, considering how awful Neb's situation had been. Had Spirit deftly dealt with the cumulative negative energy from those "excesses" on some cosmic level I wasn't privy to?

"Why," I wondered, "did Josh have to endure that tragic lifetime of loss and sorrow? Was that brief glimpse at its origin and Spirit's healing all that was needed?"

Don't Knock It, It's Working!

Almost instantly the answer to that unspoken question came through: "You don't have to know! All that matters is that the two of them… Neb and Josh… received exactly what they needed."

That simple truth was confirmed by the fact that not a single question came up in the following weeks. Josh had obviously gotten what he came for. The subtle changes in his energy and affect were proof enough that karmic blocks had effectively been released.

Eventually I settled back into my comfort zone, a bit more confident in the depth of Spirit's commitment to the work. Why, just this once, had I assumed everything had gone wrong? Was it simply because the resolution didn't suit me? I realized how silly it was to judge any outcome by my limited experience. Was this a test of faith? From somewhere deep within, a gentle voice assured me, "Things never go wrong when Spirit is in charge."

As a former intellectual snob, I had never been satisfied until I knew how things worked and why. I was convinced standard procedures were fine only if you knew exactly why they were done. Since there are exceptions to everything, it's important to know why you are doing things in a particular way. How else can you deal with the exceptions?

All my reading, studies, courses, AHP workshops, seminars and lectures taught techniques that identified various conditions and ways to successfully deal with them. There were procedures, principles, methods and techniques to determine what people needed, and to resolve the issues at hand. Gestalt, NLP, Therapeutic Touch, Core Energetics, Hypnosis, etc. all had a system of standard procedures. People studied the principles, learned the systems, and it seemed to work fine for them.

Results Trump Methodology

Working with Spirit threw all systems, theories and expectations into a cocked hat. Try as I might, I couldn't discover a pattern to the work we were doing. There was no set system, no guidelines. Yet I'd never seen such consistent, stellar results in my life.

My primary task is to help the client relax enough to enter a state of altered consciousness and then, with guided imagery, enable them to reach the destination chosen for them. After that, I have about as much influence on the session as a television set has on the programs displayed on the screen. All I can do is stay focused and channel the energy required to maintain the connection. Spirit takes over and uses my voice to communicate with the client and the incarnations we connect with. Before beginning a session I have no idea where we are going, who we will meet, what we will do there, or how to achieve the final outcome.

I get psychic flashes and impressions from time to time, but other than that I just listen to the comments and instructions coming through my mouth. As far as I know, my personal thoughts and reactions have absolutely no influence on the dramas unfolding.

In working with Spirit, the one consistent quality is mastery of any situation, no matter how challenging or complex. All clients and their alternate incarnations are treated with respect. They and their alternate incarnations are encouraged to use their own intelligence and skills in the most effective ways to heal the karmic situation. Wherever we are, Spirit adopts a language style they can relate to. Every session ends with the best possible solution. That's the one thing that's consistent throughout—positive results. With that realization, I resolved to try harder to relax and let Spirit, with infinite cosmic wisdom, work the proper miracles.

Chapter Twenty-One
A Professional Challenge

It was a rare night out. I was enjoying the full moon celebration at Alex Murray's apartment... that is, until a friend introduced me to someone she was sure I'd want to meet.

"Stephen, this is the gal I told you about who's doing such amazing things with other lifetimes," she announced. Then she turned and gravitated toward a hilarious group across the room. There was no way to escape that interrogation by the head of a New Jersey school of hypnosis. Boy, could he ask questions! They came at me machine-gun style.

"What method do you use? Who did you study with? How long have you been practicing hypnosis?"

"Sorry, Stephen, but I don't use hypnosis," I smiled.

A Difference Of Opinion

"But Millie said you're doing past life regressions," he shot back.

"Not exactly," I countered, "My sessions are not really past life regressions. We just go to another now... another place and another incarnation."

"That's past life regression. Maybe you just don't know it, but you have to be using hypnosis," he proclaimed with a touch of hubris.

"Honestly, I've never studied hypnosis. I tried hypnotic past life regression once in London and it didn't work. This is not the same."

"Look, I'm a professional," he informed me in a tone bordering on condescension. "I've been teaching hypnosis for years and I'm telling you that you're practicing hypnosis."

Rising above his bias and complacency I assured him that in my "amateur opinion" these sessions were nothing like regressions under hypnosis. "On the other hand," I continued amicably, "if I'm practicing hypnosis without knowing it, that's not so good. Would you like to sit in on a session? That way you can judge for yourself."

"That sounds like an interesting proposition," he grinned. "When would you like me to come… and where?"

"I'll call you when I have a client who is willing to allow a stranger to sit in on his or her session at my home. Is there an evening when you're usually free?"

"Wednesday is good for me," he announced with only the tiniest tinge of superiority. Convinced regression could only happen under hypnosis, he was more than certain it would be easy to prove me wrong.

"Okay, give me your card and I'll call you the first Wednesday I have a subject willing to let you sit in," I said.

As luck would have it, one of my students called to set up an appointment the following Wednesday. I asked if she'd mind if the head of a School of Hypnosis sat in on her session.

"What an amusing concept," she giggled. "Why not? It might be rather interesting."

I called Stephen with the news. He was delighted.

For my part, it was not all that delightful. The prospect of working under professional scrutiny was daunting.

Silent Witness

Wednesday evening he and Lili arrived simultaneously. I introduced them to each other and prepared for the session. Stephen observed my preparations without comment. I was quite aware that he thought candles and incense were redundant. It didn't seem necessary to edify him as to their purpose. The energy vibrations they emanate facilitate the work. The only reason I allowed him to observe was to determine whether or not hypnosis was involved in my work.

Lili was a wonderful subject. My spiritual development students were accustomed to dealing with Spirit. We had built a solid community of harmony and trust.

Stephen moved a chair directly behind me, the better to observe my work. Even if I had not been "out of it" I would not have been able to judge his reactions.

Once the process began, Spirit took over and, as usual, brought the situation into focus and provided guidance to resolve the issues at hand. This was not one of our more dramatic confrontations, but I thought it went quite well. As I guided Lili back into the 20th century, Stephen cleared his throat. When I was able, I turned to him inquiringly.

Our professional observer was leaning half out of his chair in excitement.

"I've got two comments," he announced.

Lili and I were all ears.

Professional Confirmation

"Number one," Stephen counted on his fingers, "It's definitely not hypnosis; she was not under your control."

Lili reached out, touched my hand gently and grinned.

"You were so positive it was hypnosis, Stephen," I responded, "what made you change your mind? How do you know for sure?"

"By the mistakes you made." he chuckled.

"Mistakes?"

"Look," he explained in his School of Hypnosis Director voice, "under hypnosis she would have had to agree with every suggestion you made. For example, if she were hypnotized and you had said, 'Isn't this a beautiful red rug?' even though she had been looking right at it, she would have agreed that it was a lovely red rug. If you had suggested that to this woman, she would have said, 'Are you blind or crazy? Can't you see that's a gray rug?' So you see, it couldn't be hypnosis."

To the best of my knowledge, that made our sessions officially unique in the "past life regression" category. But before I had time to absorb it, he upped the ante.

"Number two," he grinned, "Me next!"

So what's a girl to do? Graciously oblige, of course.

Stephen and Lili changed places. I looked at her and gestured toward the door. She shook her head, not about to miss this one.

Stephen's trip to another lifetime was quite amusing. Lili and I couldn't help giggling At one point the callow youth we were visiting with complained sulkily, "You're laughing at me!"

"No, no," Lili assured him, "We're not laughing at you, we're laughing with you. You're very cute."

When Stephen came back to "normal consciousness," he pronounced it a remarkable experience. "But you did laugh at me," he grumbled. "I vividly remember every single word and everything that happened even though you didn't bother to give me a post-hypnotic suggestion to remember. It all felt so very normal… so real."

"There ya go!" I laughed. "Are you glad you came?"

He nodded vigorously and looked around for his coat.

After seeing the two of them out I sat down to analyze the evening's events. Stephen's determination to prove me wrong had turned out to be a gift in disguise. Now what?

Counting the Ways

Stephen's professional critique should have ended all doubts. He had confirmed that what I now called *Multi-Life Therapy* was a technique completely separate from hypnosis. Instead of relief at having passed the test with flying colors, I felt an increased sense of responsibility.

"What has Spirit gotten me into?" I asked the empty room. For the first time, it seemed important to "face the facts" in order to better define this work that had taken over my life.

Years of denying and/or ignoring my healing ability to no avail had convinced me there was no way to dodge the bullet. It was only 11:45 pm. I might as well begin now before the magnitude of it all sends me into a state of paralysis. The longer I put it off, the harder it will be. Okay, this is different from hypnotic regressions… but how? It might help to have a comparison chart. I grabbed a legal pad and pen and began a checklist.

HYPNOSIS	MULTI-LIFE THERAPY
1. Hypnotist in command	Client makes the choices
2. Observe past events	Visit and interact with the other incarnation(s)
3. Relive painful events	Painless by prior agreement
4. Nothing can be changed because it's all in the past	Create new, better outcome making wiser decisions with nformation provided by Spirit
5. Analyze information	Issues brought out in the session and resolved are life changing
6. Ongoing psychotherapy.	Cosmic revitalization at end of session recharges client.

Unresolved Questions

That's a start, but there's more. I began a second list to address my own questions about *Multi-Life Therapy*.

- *How is it possible for karma to just melt away—and years, even centuries of karmic blockage be eliminated?*
- *Why does it seem so natural and normal to talk with a "past" incarnation in their world?*
- *How could anyone live 21, or maybe even 50 years beyond their original death date?*
- *What happens to children and grandchildren of someone who originally died childless?*
- *Is it normal for different incarnations to alternate between male and female, powerful and weak, black and white, retarded and brilliant, poor and rich?*
- *Why have we never encountered a "famous" person, like Napoleon or Cleopatra?*
- *Why does genealogy seem to be the least important part of the equation?* [7]

When I was on my own, it was not all that simple. My lists left me with more questions than answers. During the sessions, everything seemed so easy—with nothing to fear or question. There was always a Spirit (or angel) on our side to guide clients and their alternate incarnations through rough waters, protect and support them, meanwhile pulling off miracles right and left.

Uncomfortable as my role of observer may be, it is not without its priceless rewards. In every session I have watched Spirit in action, crafting solutions that would confound the world's greatest strategists. My faith in the limitless good will and compassion of "The Creator of All That Is" (God for short) has constantly been reconfirmed. I am humbled and amazed at the beauty and adaptability of the immortal human spirit.

One thing for sure, this work is more a shortcut for success,

---

[7] *Stardust just nudged me as I proofed the manuscript and answered that question. She says, "Because the soul isn't tied to or limited by biology—that's Earth stuff. DNA cellular memories are useful for survival on this plane."*

as opposed to a change, which could go either way. It takes faith and commitment. Spirit doesn't wave a magic wand and make everything fall perfectly into place. The people we meet must make their own choices and work hard to overcome their challenges. It takes courage and determination to face the unknown and persevere through hardship to a new outcome. The reward is a future with fewer obstacles and less bad karma in both lives: there and here.

I suspect what we've learned so far is only the tip of the iceberg. How changes in these lifetimes create such miracles in our current lives is still a mystery to me. Karma is far more powerful and complex than logic can explain. Attempts to rationalize so many unknown possibilities scramble the brain. Maybe tomorrow it will all make more sense. For now I'll settle for just knowing.

Chapter Twenty-Two
Into The Dark Side

Kitty, a petite blonde aspiring actress, had been a regular in our spiritual development classes for some time before she got the courage to explore another lifetime. She arrived under a full head of steam. Alone for the first time, she took center stage. Eyes shining like klieg lights, she vibrated with expectation. Relaxation techniques were attacked with such passionate fervor it was a small miracle the couch stayed put.

It was daunting. I wondered if she would ever be able to reach the peaceful, relaxed state necessary to enter the requisite state of altered consciousness.

The Method

Her first attempt could only be compared to a silent movie version of an insomniac fighting desperately to fall asleep. She really worked the assignment.

"This might as well be a theatrical scene rehearsal," I thought to myself. "First we have to get past 'the method'… but how?" I was getting nowhere.

The distress signals must have been urgent because Spirit arrived and immediately took charge. "You're just perfect the way you are. You don't have to try so hard. Just melt into a puddle of butterscotch pudding," came through my lips.

It seemed a peculiar image to use as a calming tactic, but odd or not, it worked. I settled back for what might well be a very interesting trip.

"Turn off the thinking machine and just be," Spirit continued.

"The only way you can interfere with the process is by thinking too much. Just breathe… and float softly on the breath."

"Sounds like that was meant for both of us," I told myself. It was time to put analytical faculties on hold and get out of the way.

The tense little body on the couch slowly succumbed to the rhythmic cadence, the melodic timbre of voice and the peaceful yet powerful presence emanating from Spirit.

"Talk about making an almost impossible task seem easy," I thought to myself, "Wow!"

The Village Market

When Kitty finally let go of her acting techniques she drifted into a setting that could only be Medieval Europe. It was a seething mass of roiling humanity. The jostling crowd overflowed into narrow cobblestoned streets. I suppressed a giggle. This was either a Cecil B. DeMille set, a Bruegel painting come to life, or a medieval open market.

"Ugh! I've never seen anything so grubby, filthy, grimy and, ooh, the smell," Kitty squealed. "Who are these… these awful people? This is disgusting! There are thieves all over the place… and the shopkeepers aren't any better. What are we doing here?"

My left hemisphere was at it again, "Petty thieves and villainous shopkeepers—Dickens would have had a field day here!" I caught myself and refocused into listening mode.

All Kitty wanted to do was to get as far away as possible from this ambulatory garbage pit. "Oh my god, she gasped, "The filth, the overpowering stench, the coarseness of this milling crowd."

With infinite patience, our cosmic tour guide endeavored to shift Kitty's awareness past revulsion on the physical level and into a more spiritual realm. "You have come here for a purpose. Now it is necessary to seek out the one person in this crowd with whom you can identify."

Guiding her through this emotional cauldron to tune in to one single soul energy was a formidable task. Spirit stuck to basics. The soft and easy yet unrelenting approach eased her past disgust and loathing. "Look down and tell me what is on your feet," came the patient guidance.

At first she couldn't see anything, but answers to simple questions revealed a 30-year-old male walking in the market.

"Can you tell me where this market is… what village? I'm a stranger here," Spirit inquired.

"Nottingham?" Kitty almost choked in disbelief.

Easing gently past this sticking point, Spirit prompted encouragingly, "Thank you. What year is it?"

Dead silence. Kitty's head moved slightly from side to side in the manner of a person confused by a question.

"That's fine, it's just now. By what name are you called?"

"I don't know. I really don't know. All I'm getting is a feeling," Kitty mumbled.

"That's perfect. Are these people around you friends, foes or neither?"

"They're criminals! They're all cheats! They cheat at cards, at dice… and they smell like a sewer. They're all wet. It's raining and they're not even getting clean. They just smell awful."

Now that Kitty was fully engaged, Spirit confided that we were from another country and asked the young man to take us to his home. "We've come as friends, to help you in any way we can. Will you trust us?"

"Yes, but who are you?"

"Kitty is a soul sister, another part of your own soul. I am a helper," Spirit explained.

A Humble Abode

Kitty's voice took on a deeper tone as she described the humble dwelling. "It's an old, thatched, half-tumbled-down building. And there's straw on the floor. Lots of mist and smoke."

"Is the smoke from a fireplace?" Spirit inquired.

"No fireplace. Fire's in the center of the room. It is on a stone."

"How does the smoke get out?"

"Through a hole in the top of the roof. And the rain… it rains in. It's bright even though the day is gray," he explained.

"Is this your home?"

"It's where he lives," Kitty interjected, "and where he works. He stays there. There are horses too."

"The horses are outside?"

"Yes, it's not really a building; it's a sort of roof they're under… and there's straw everywhere…"

"A lean-to, perhaps?" Spirit prompted.

"And the horses are tethered," she continued.

"Do you live alone, sir?" Spirit cleverly diverted Kitty, focusing on the strong male presence.

"No," came his monosyllabic response.

"How many people live here with you?

"Not many, just family. But other people come and visit."

I took a breath of relief, knowing that Spirit had finally established a solid connection.

"There's a female, feels like his wife," Kitty blurted. "Beautiful auburn hair… long… hanging down her back."

"By what name do you call your wife, my friend?"

"I call her Honey. That's her name."

"And what does she call you?"

"Not a name…. it's more of a nickname. She calls me Beast."

"You are her lovable beast, I see."

"She's tiny!" Kitty interrupted, unable to resist the role of commentator. "She's so tiny and he's so very, very big… and he's hairy. He's got huge forearms and dirty fingernails. He's really big!"

"Almost a giant?"

Kitty's head bobbed enthusiastically. "Brown hair. I can see the hair. And she has really, really red hair and very green eyes. She's beautiful. She's wearing dark brown. There's a white cloth over her hair. It's not a shawl. It's stiffer, like linen. I don't know how it stays in place… it just sort of sticks up there. Oh, and now I can see what's on his feet. He's wearing really heavy leather shoes, like work boots."

"And what work does he do?"

"The horses… it's something to do with horses. I think he's a blacksmith."

"Did you say 'he' or 'I'?"

"I… he… and it's all for her… she's a good woman."

Once we had confirmed that this minus five foot, dainty female was connected to the hulking good-natured giant, the impressions came fast and clear.

"He is obviously a good man who's under tremendous pressure," she explained.

"He? Try just saying 'I,'" Spirit urged.

"I… he… she doesn't want him to go out."

A Dangerous Mistake

Kitty was uneasy in her bubble. This was her soul brother and she sensed trouble. "He's on the verge of a terrible mistake. He's good, but on the wrong track. She doesn't want him to go but he says he must. He promised them."

"Where are you going? Whom did you promise to meet?"

"There's some kind of meeting."

When Spirit took us forward in time it felt dangerous. No matter how desperate his circumstances, Kitty did not want him there.

"He shouldn't be doing this at all!" she muttered. "I think he's with," she groped for the right term. "He's with—uhh… there are trees all around and it's dark and they're all wearing black. It must be a coven. The leader greeted him as 'brother,' but he's not happy to be here. He's angry. Why is he here?" Jumbled, run-on sentences marked the depth of her concern.

"Stop trying to analyze the situation and just be. You mustn't pass judgment, Spirit urged. "Let us help this man."

"Okay, okay," she muttered grimly, with a sigh of resignation.

"Why is he angry?" Spirit prompted.

"Because Honey told him he's doing the wrong thing?" she ventured. "Because she's right?"

With infinite cosmic awareness, Spirit responded, "Yes, but there's more."

"…and he's angry," Kitty volunteered, "because she's so beautiful and he loves her so. It's all for her. He wants to take good care of her, to please her so badly. He wishes she'd understand," she sighed.

Rapid eye movements and grimaces told me she had finally merged fully with the gentle giant and understood what was troubling him. The energy pouring through her reminded me of Samson chained to the pillars of the temple. The transformation was so sudden and complete it left me breathless. Beast's raw pain swallowed her completely.

"But Honey just doesn't understand," a rough male voice broke through. At last Spirit could communicate directly with this troubled man.

"What doesn't she understand?" Spirit asked.

"How good it can be?"

"How good what can be?"

"The power."

"What power?" Spirit demanded.

"Uh… it's just 'the power,'" he muttered.

"What kind of power… power over what or whom? Tell me what it is that convinced you this is the right thing to do? What has lured you here? Why do you believe their spells and potions can make your life so much better?" came the gentle, insistent barrage of questions.

"They say you can rule men with power," he whispered. "You can get things with power. That's why I want to do it… so I can use the power to get everything Honey's due."

In my leftish bubble perch I paid very close attention. The picture grew clearer by the minute. My heart went out to this victim of poverty and societal limitations.

"So you only want the power they promised you to get the things you want to give to Honey," Spirit summed up.

"He wants to give her such simple things…" Kitty blurted, "things it would be unthinkable to live without in the twentieth century."

"Those small things are his definition of power," I reflected privately.

Kitty's body language spoke volumes. She was now fully engaged in the battle against evil. "We've got to do whatever it takes to help him!" she announced in her own well-rounded tones.

The well-intentioned but very confused young hulk of a man needed all the help he could get to avoid making an irrevocable mistake. Now Spirit, Kitty and I were united in a campaign to talk him out of further involvement with this dangerous cult.

"Please, Beast, don't do this terrible thing," Kitty pleaded.

"But I gave my word as a man. A man's got to live up to his word," Beast responded passionately.

"Bartholomew," the wise Spirit voice argued, "I don't think you understand what these people are really about. They are about power, that's true, but it's their power, not yours. They may give you a token here and there, but you'll pay a thousand times over for the little bits they give you."

That got my attention! I could not recall ever hearing anything but the nickname, "Beast." Add one more anomaly to ponder upon. What else was Spirit privy to?

"But they're looking at me," he protested. "I told them I was going to become a part of their circle. I can't back down, can I?" He wrestled with his conscience, his very manhood.

"How will Spirit handle this dilemma?" I wondered. There must be a way to convince him his honor will be more at peril if he doesn't get out of there fast. We were pitted against the man's self-image, his own peculiar code of honor.

"No sacrifice is too great!" he stoutly averred. "I must do what'ere I can to get food and warm clothes and a decent place to live for my family… for Honey and the babe."

Spirit to the Rescue

"You must get away from these people. They will force you to do wicked things that will bring shame upon you and your family," Spirit chanted loudly. "They will destroy your honor for all eternity!"

That pronouncement came out with such conviction that Bartholomew gasped in horror. Truth he'd half-suspected but had managed to ignore hit home like a physical blow. Once that truth was accepted, all objections were forgotten. The consequences of his impetuous decision came flooding through in full force.

"How can I get away?" he whispered. "They're expecting me. They'll know something is wrong."

"What do you think they might do then?"

"They might hurt me. They might hurt my wife!" His voice rose as he became overwrought with distress.

Spirit offered a simple solution. "Bartholomew, tell the leader of the coven that you have forgotten something… your pouch, perhaps."

Kitty's body squirmed uncomfortably. Her right hand went to her hip and patted it, indicating that he had his pouch with him. That meant he'd have to tell a lie… something that was against his code of honor.

"I… I don't know if they'll believe me."

"You must have forgotten something… some token they told you to bring…" Spirit offered.

"A kerchief… Honey's kerchief! I forgot it, but it's so silly…"

"Not silly at all. Her kerchief is what they need to give them power over her, too. Then they could do whatever they want with her! You must convince them your excuse is legitimate! Tell them quickly and leave. Come with us… now!" Spirit commanded.

He wavered uncertainly, looking furtively from side to side.

"Come with Kitty and me… now! We have something very important to show you."

With our urging he made his excuse, saying truthfully that he'd forgotten the kerchief and must go back for it.

"Take my hand, Bartholomew, and walk away now. I will show you power far greater than this whole coven can muster," promised our guide.

My hand lifted automatically and reached out of its own accord to grasp the hand he offered. I felt an electrical charge shoot down my arm into Kitty-Bartholomew's hand.

"He's smiling… he's smiling!" Kitty gloated.

Spirit led him to a great gnarled white oak tree. "Come to this sacred tree with me. Take off your shoes and lean back against its trunk. Join forces with this powerful, ancient tree spirit and with God, who reaches out to us through nature."

As instructed, Bartholomew removed his shoes, leaned his body against the trunk. As he touched in with the great spirit of the tree, he sighed deeply.

"Feel yourself at one with nature," Spirit declaimed. "Those fools lied to you when they told you that they could rule over the forces of nature. That's all they have to offer—lies and tricks. Power struggles against nature never work. You must work in harmony with God, becoming one with the true spiritual forces of nature, instead of pitting your strength against them. Take a deep breath and release your pent-up anger. Let it go with each breath, again… again. There. Feel yourself being filled with the power of endless love." The voice rose a bit, confident, persuasive and oh so effective.

The positive power of nature permeated his whole being. Bartholomew fell silent, trembling with the effort to accept a new, foreign way of thinking. Gamely he struggled to grasp a concept undreamt-of in his time.

In my little corner of consciousness I cheered him on. Was it possible for this man of the Dark Ages to believe he could be powerful without joining a black warlocks' coven?

"I tremble when I think of the terrible vengeance the brothers of the coven wreak upon those who defy them," he whispered.

"You are safe. The sacred power of the Almighty overcomes and ultimately destroys all who boast of their wickedness," Spirit proclaimed in resonant tones.

Pledge of Honor

In the cadence and vernacular of the era, Spirit issued his challenge: "Pledge your homage now, Bartholomew, or bow to the pretenders. Will your allegiance be to the power of light and goodness, or to the power of darkness? Do you choose to labor for evil or for good? Pledge your heart and hand to the power worthy of your loyalty."

"I, Bartholomew, pledge homage to the forces of good, forever forsaking the path of the Evil One," Kitty intoned passionately, hand pressed tightly to her heart.

Bartholomew was free from an irrevocable commitment to the path of evil. A wave of relief washed over me.

Clear, precise instructions issued forth from Spirit: "Call upon the forces of Good. Gather them to you and surround yourself with the invisible shield I entrust to you. It will protect you from all evil forces."

"Take it, Beast. It works!" Kitty whispered fiercely.

Bye Bye Bad Karma

Gradually, with Kitty's support and the quiet conviction of our Spirit guide, Bartholomew began to accept that the forces of good were available to him as needed. A lifetime of artificial constraints had yet to be surmounted.

"How will we live? We can barely survive on the bits and bobs I make as a blacksmith," he pointed out mournfully. "It's not enough to keep the two of us warm and fed. We barely keep body and soul together. My wife is with child. How can I support my family in this hardscrabble world?" he mumbled uncertainly.

Spirit, drawing on intimate knowledge of his life, offered an ingenious plan. "You know how to ride a horse don't you?"

Kitty's head bobbed in confirmation.

"You are well trained in the field of combat, correct?"

Again, he nodded eagerly. "I used to practice the manly arts with the son of the lord. We used to be fine friends. We grew up together."

"You can use those skills to earn whatever you need, Bartholomew. It is time to put your great heart and your strong arm to good use. Your prowess with sword and lance will make your wife proud to stand by your side."

"But dare I? Folk like me had best not reach too high. Tis dangerous."

"With your powerful body and your quick reflexes, you can win any jousting tournament you enter," Spirit insisted.

Bartholomew gasped at the magnitude of a concept that would never have occurred to one entrapped on the lower rung of a caste society.

"But how can I begin? I know of no one who would… or even could… sponsor me in such a tournament."

"You have the skills to craft your own armor. Do so, and present yourself at the royal jousting tournament, running at full tilt on the fine mount you own. The time is nearing. You had best prepare yourself."

"My wife is in prayer, hoping to sway me from my folly. She will gladly fashion a banner for me… and proper garments," Bartholomew beamed.

Time spun away at whirlwind pace, leaving me in awe.

Bartholomew was faithful to his promise. He followed the instructions precisely. Grunts, sighs and heavy breathing marked the intensity of his efforts.

Kitty kept us abreast of his progress. The armor was lovingly crafted, jousting exercises undertaken, a coat of arms fashioned, and all was ready in time for the tournament.

"Ooh, you should see how splendid he looks," Kitty crowed.

Triumphant Entry

Spirit, with total mastery of the theatrics and etiquette of medieval tourneys, held Bartholomew in waiting until the perfect moment for his flamboyant entry. He exploded into the arena, circled the field with dramatic flair and skidded to a halt with a grand salute and oath of fealty to his king.

Bye Bye Bad Karma

Once in the fray, he held sway with his mighty arm. All eyes were glued to his lightning moves. His distinctive armor was like nothing seen before. The king, mesmerized by the daring moves of the mysterious outsider, cheered him on. Bartholomew won every combat. At the end of the tourney he knelt before the king to receive his favor and the purse pledged to the winner.

The fame and rewards from that one tournament alone guaranteed a far better future than Bartholomew could have imagined. Fears of providing for his wife and child were behind him.

"And now, let's go to the end of that very rewarding future you've just earned. Go to the moment when you break free from your body, leaving earthly cares behind."

Such an enormous sigh ripped through Kitty's small frame I thought she was going to fly off the couch.

"Look upon the woman called Kitty. Know that she, your soul sister, has fought valiantly to save you from folly. Acknowledge her fierce defense of your honor and her determination to see you through. Looking deeply into her life path, you will find invisible strings of guilt stretching back to that momentary capitulation you have now burned out of your consciousness forever. You can now honor her deep loyalty to you and return the favor. There will be future times when she will need to be reminded of how powerful she is. Lend her your spirit, your enhanced wisdom and strength. Drink deep from the ewer of wisdom bestowed upon you by angelic beings and tell her what she needs to hear now."

"I guess it's of her world, and I really don't understand it," he hesitated, "but I'll say it word by word. Walk softly and carry a big stick."

A resounding "Aah" signaled Kitty's understanding. Bartholomew apparently took it as his cue to dash headlong into his own version of paradise.

Kitty came out of that session armed with the best advice a triumphant, confident version of Bartholomew could give.

Once back in this particular "here and now," she couldn't gather her things together fast enough.

"I need privacy to mull things over… to sort and re-sort that close encounter with evil," she blurted.

I really couldn't blame her. Outsmarting black warlocks' covens took a lot out of one. I was exhausted and I had only gone along for the ride! I hugged her and sent her on her way, more than certain that she and Bartholomew would make the most of the events they'd shared tonight.

A second after the door closed she knocked. I thought perhaps she'd forgotten something, but it was just the opposite. She leaned around the edge of the door and giggled, "I just remembered. How did you know butterscotch pudding is my all-time favorite?"

Duh! I shrugged, grinned and gave her one more hug.

Results… and More

Whether Kitty used "the method," or just waited until the drama seeped into her internal version of reality was quite unimportant. By whatever means and methods available, she sorted it all out and used the information wisely.

Gradually all the guilt, self-doubt and sense of futility accumulated long centuries ago within that circle of black warlocks fell away. Bartholomew's catastrophic capitulation to the forces of evil (now completely erased from her core consciousness) could hold her back no longer. Unburdened and free of a bunch of negative karma, she ably set forth to achieve her own goals.

Kitty found a new acting coach and threw herself into a heavy schedule of classes. A few months later she called to tell me she had decided to change her name to one more appropriate for a professional actress. Watch out world. This tiny ball of energy is coming at you full tilt.

Even though her overloaded schedule left no room for class,

she managed to keep in touch. Occasional calls kept me up to date with the latest steps she had taken in her career—the new scene partner, the new coach, the new agent—increasing confidence and the recognition she received.

Spiritual Lessons Gratefully Acknowledged

When clients call or stop by to tell me about the benefits they've reaped from their sessions, it fills my heart to overflowing. Truth be told, they were not the only ones who profited from this work. As weeks go by, I gain profound spiritual knowledge from witnessing Spirit in action. What I learned during Kitty's trip to "Sherwood Forest," as she called it, is beyond measure. I'll share:

> - *Prayers alone cannot prevent loved ones from making rash mistakes. Sometimes you have to chase them down and shake some sense into them… in other words, pray as if it all depends on God, and act as if it all depends on you.*
> - *A dramatic rescue from disastrous peril drives home a lesson far more powerfully than any lecture, pleading or logic.*
> - *Nothing can beat a chance to preview probable results of impulsive actions. Virtual foresight makes it easy to choose a better path and avoid unnecessary pain.*
> - *It's not necessary to re-live the pain and torture resulting from bad choices in order to learn from the mistakes made in lifetimes we visit.*
> - *Each incarnation is free to either cling to an old belief and suffer, or take Spirit's advice and use it to create a better outcome.*
> - *Spirit encourages but does not coerce anyone into taking actions against their will, even for their own good.*
> - *Each incarnation must fully acknowledge and accept their own power to create a bright new future instead of*

repeating the old choices. When trust is established, Spirit can carve a new path around any disaster and eliminate the after effects of the original event. All that's required is faith, teamwork and a little Spirit magic.

In short, re-writing history seems to be a fool-proof formula for eliminating residual effects of the recurring karmic contrail that persists, incarnation after incarnation. What a revelation! Even karma accrued from selling one's soul to the devil can be completely erased—integrity restored and residual negative energy patterns permanently erased. The life that unfolds after making new enlightened choices is permanently embedded in the core consciousness. I was giddy as a teenager with a brand new "profound truth."

Chapter Twenty-Three
A Bridge to Transformation

The guy who slipped quietly into my living room seemed too conservative to fit the profile of the usual voyager. Roger obviously didn't share my concern as to the outcome. Seriously, as if about to mount a witness stand, he listened to my now standard overview and guidance orientation. Nodding solemnly, he indicated his readiness to begin and settled onto the couch.

With surprising ease he negotiated the relaxation phase. A contented sigh followed by soft, shallow breathing told me he had arrived at the destination Spirit knew to be most important for him to deal with right now.

I asked where he was and he said he was floating in the air, hovering over a vessel in the middle of the ocean. He described it as a very ordinary kind of ship, not modern or well kept.

"Can you describe the soul brother or sister you've come to visit with?"

"Just a regular guy, kinda quiet… looks a bit out of place on the ship. He's no sailor, that's for sure."

Obtaining permission for him to speak through Roger, I introduced myself and explained I'd come to befriend him in any way that would be helpful.

"Hmm… guess I could use a friend, that's the truth," he responded.

When asked about himself, he said, "Call me Pat," and volunteered that he was married with two children.

"Are they here with you?"

"No!" he responded with a short, bitter laugh.

"Sounds like you're not happy about that." I responded, idly wondering where Spirit could be.

"Sometimes ye're forced to make sacrifices t'better yer life."

"That takes courage."

"True enough, that!" he grunted.

The Limerick

Asked about the ship, all he knew about it was its name, the Limerick, and its destination—America.

"How did you get on this ship?"

"Sold animals fer the price o' me passage."

"How are your wife and children going to live while you are away?"

"They must depend upon others for assistance, God help 'em."

"What are your plans?"

"I'll work and send 'em money."

"Where will you live when you get to America?"

"With my cousin Ed."

"Let's go forward in time to your life in America. Tell me what is happening."

"We're working on a bridge."

"We?"

"Yes. My cousin 'n me."

"What kind of work are you doing on the bridge?"

"Construction (grunt); gettin' it ready for the big ships to come through," came the laconic response. Pat was a man of few words.

A Bridge to Tranformation

"What bridge are you working on?" I inquired.

"Brooklyn."

"How interesting! Can you tell me what year it is?"

"1912."

Bye Bye Bad Karma

That date didn't match my version of history, so I asked, "What kind of work are you doing on this bridge?"
"Digging under the river.[8]"
"Kind of dangerous work, isn't it?"
"Yes, but the pay's good."
"How much are they paying you?"
"Two dollars a day."
"Is that a lot of money for you?"
"Yes."
"Where are you living?"
"Right down on the waterfront."
"How long have you been working on the bridge?"
"Three weeks."
"Have you managed to save some money?"

---

[8] *In 1912 The East River Project, based on Col. Wm. E. Black's Channel Survey, deepened the East River to 35 ft. Most of the work was done by immigrants, primarily Irish, called Sandhogs.*

"Not yet. I'm payin' rent… and payin' back the money I borrowed from my cousin."

"When you get that debt paid off and the money's your own, what will you do with it?"

"I'll be sending it back to me family."

"You're a good man, Pat."

The grunt might have been an answer… but then it could have been from the effort of digging. His body movements indicated rhythmic effort. This was not a man to be diverted from his work and I was running out of ideas.

Spirit smoothly took charge. Apparently I'd done well enough so far that he hadn't felt needed. I suspected things were about to get interesting.

"Let us go forward in time to the next important thing that happens to you, Pat," Spirit suggested. "Tell me what's happening, please."

The War to End War

"It's the war," came the muffled reply.

"What war?"

"The War to End War," he announced solemnly.

The voice was different, I noticed. It was more confident and the thick Irish brogue was less pronounced. "It must have changed during his years in America," I thought to myself. Spirit was moving on, so I stopped indulging in idle speculation.

"What year is it?" Spirit inquired.

"1917."

"Where is your family?"

"In America."

"Where are you living right now?"

"In a tent."

"A tent?" Spirit's guiding questions matched Pat's brevity.

An army tent."

"Who am I speaking with?" Spirit asked, possibly to resolve my uncertainty.

"My name is Josh!"

Boy, was I confused. "What happened to Pat? It was 1912 when we were at the dredging site with Pat and this was only five years later." My mind was running amok. "Could this be an overlapping incarnation, or was Pat a catchall nickname for Irishmen?" Questions piled up with no answer. "Ah, never mind… the client is more important," my left brain rattled on. "Down girl," I admonished myself. "Stop that mind chatter. Spirit knows exactly how to handle anything and everything, right?"

"Where are we now?" Spirit, undisturbed by my confusion, continued the quest for information.

"France," he grunted.

"Why are you here?"

"Army brought me here."

"What is your rank?"

"Corporal."

"And what do they call you, corporal?"

"They call me by my name—Corporal Hokum."

"How long have you been here in France?"

"Six months."

"What outfit are you with?"

"125th Infantry."

That was interesting. In the little corner of my mind I made a note to check and see if there was such a company in WWI.

"Who is the leader of the 125th Infantry?"

"General Pierce."

"What is the most important thing in your life right now?"

"Danger."

"Did you volunteer or were you drafted?"

"Volunteered."

"Why did you volunteer?"
"To get a bonus, money for my family."
"How old are you, Josh?"
"Thirty-one."

That threw me into a bit of mathematical confusion… but right brain orientation makes it almost impossible to calculate dates, ages, names and locations. It's always a challenge in these forays into alternate reality. Once again I forced myself to set curiosity aside. Time progression is insignificant compared to the soul issues we came here to resolve.

Influenza!

Unperturbed by my attempts at orientation, Spirit moved on easily, "Let us go forward in time to the next important thing that happens to you, Josh. Tell me what's happening."
"My wife's funeral."
"That must be hard for you. Where is your wife being buried?"
"New York."
"What caused her death?"
"Influenza, I think that's what they called it… the flu epidemic."
"What year is it?"
"1924[9]."
"What are you going to do now, Josh?"
"Nothing to do but just keep on working."
"What kind of work are you doing?"
"Mechanic."
"Where do you work?"
"Mike's Garage… it's in Chelsea."
"How old are your children?"
"One's 14 and the other's 10."

---

[9] The US Department of Commerce reported the flu epidemic death toll was 1,173,990. Total US population was under 100 million.

"It must be hard for a working man alone with two children.
"Who takes care of them?"
"Flora, my cousin's wife."
"It's good to have family to count on, right? Let's go forward again in time to the next important thing that happens to you.
"I'm in the Veterans' Hospital."
"What are you here for?"
"Cancer… it's my lungs."
"Do you smoke cigarettes?"
"Yes."

I couldn't resist putting my two cents in: "It's not known in your time, but cigarettes are one of the main causes of lung cancer. Tell your children not to smoke."

"I'll do that," Josh responded solemnly, "wouldn't want them to suffer what I'm going through."

"Good," Spirit blithely resumed. "Now let's go forward in time to your last day on earth as Josh Hokum and tell me what is happening. Where are you?"

"In the hospital… still," he gasped in a squeaky voice.
"What year is it?"
"1928."
"Do you know this is your last day on Earth?"
"Yes."

"Josh, you've paid your dues. You don't need to be in pain any longer. Float out of your body and into freedom," Spirit confidently instructed. The tortured breathing eased within seconds. "And now that you've released your spirit from that pain-racked body," Spirit continued, "allow yourself to float away from it. Let go of the pain, poverty and loss you've lived with. Let it go. Reach out to the greater part of your soul, and renew your connection with that wholeness. Now you will find you are able to look forward and backward in time. You are reconnecting with the wisdom of the ages… the power that we all have to give up in order to come into human form. Tell me, please, why you chose to be born as a poor Irish farmer?"

Time Between Time

Roger's face registered a range of expressions that would make any actor envious: relief, surprise, contemplation and peace. It finally settled into a composed visage of gentle strength and confidence. His answer came in a greatly altered voice.

"To help the poor people. To be with them."

"Who did you want to be with? Anyone that you had known before?"

"My wife."

"In what other lifetime did you know her?"

"In Egypt," came the half questioning, half wondering response.

"Who was she to you then?"

"My second wife… my favorite."

"What did you do in that lifetime in Egypt that made you choose to punish yourself, as you seem to have been doing ever since?" Spirit inquired.

"I was hungry for power. And… and… I stole her. I shouldn't have done that. I could have been killed."

At Spirit's prompting, he confessed that he had stolen her from Tzaheer, a Ja-ling High Priest. She was only sixteen.

"What was she doing with the priest?"

"She was a maid."

Theft or Liberation?

Spirit's questioning determined that he was kind to her, and she was happy being with him. "Then why do you feel guilty about stealing her? You must rid yourself of that sense of guilt right now. Release it… let it go," Spirit's voice rose with absolute authority.

"God is not punishing you. No one is punishing you except yourself. Know that right now!"

"He put a curse on me!" he whispered.

"Who did? The priest?"

He swallowed heavily and gulped, "Uh huh!"

"Understand something," the Spirit voice took on more power and resonance, "it is very important that you know this. The primary law of the universe is the Law of Cause and Effect. 'That which you send out you will receive back increased and multiplied.' In cursing you the priest actually cursed himself. You will only suffer from his curse as long as you surrender your will to his. Can you see that?"

"Yes."

"Are you willing to forgive yourself for liberating your wife from slavery?"

"Yes."

"Now to the other things you blame yourself for in that lifetime. Let us discuss the deeds for which you punish yourself. You said you were hungry for power."

"Yes, that's right."

"Why did you want that power?"

"For the prestige and the privileges power gave me."

"I see. Do you believe you misused that power? Did you hurt anyone?"

"The priest was a holy man and I discredited him."

"How did you go about that?"

"I told lies about him."

"What kind of lies?"

"I said he stole money."

"Was he in a position to help a lot of people?"

"Yes."

"And you feel that by lying about him you prevented that from happening. Is that what you mean?"

"Yes."

"Then we must ask forgiveness from him. Call his name three times and he will appear before you."

Fearfully, hesitantly he whispered, "Tzaheer… Tzaheer… Tzaheer."

"He is here now, right?"

"Ohh…"

"You have the opportunity, here and now, to ask his forgiveness. Do so."

"Thank you," he mumbled and drew a ragged breath. "Tzaheer, I humbly beg you to forgive me for the untruths I spoke against you. I am truly sorry."

Roger cringed as if to ward off an expected blow.

"Listen carefully," Spirit prompted. "Tell us how he responds to your sincere apology and request for forgiveness."

In the profound silence, I marveled at this new aspect of *Multi-Life Therapy*. Never before had an incarnation we visited faced an enemy from another incarnation in an attempt to resolve a karmic debt. This was totally new—an opportunity to apologize for an offense between lifetimes!

Ethereal Pardon

In a reverential tone Roger reported, "He's smiling! He says, 'Old friend, I see that you have subjected yourself to much unnecessary torture. But what have you learned? In the spirit world I now inhabit we do not believe in torture; nor do we believe in revenge.'"

Spirit added a mild commentary. "I suspect Tzaheer had been somewhat too arrogant in his power… his holiness, over in Egypt. He has learned much and changed greatly in the spirit world. He now reaches out to you from that level of consciousness. Don't be afraid. Let him place his hand upon your brow. This gesture is his formal confirmation of forgiveness."

"He's telling me—he's charging me with the responsibility to use my power for good."

"To have power and to refuse to put it to good use is a sin. Do you understand that?" Spirit kindly inquired.

"Yes."

"And you have not been using your power. Is this not correct? You have paid more than tenfold for the sins you committed in that Egyptian lifetime. Give yourself permission to be free—right now!"

That came through with such force that I was startled into wondering if it might also be meant for me.

"I give myself permission to be free," Roger intoned softly.

"Give yourself, now and henceforth, permission to behold and enjoy the beauty of life… to do everything you're capable of doing for the remainder of your current life. Give yourself permission to earn, to spend, and to have money. Money in and of itself is not evil. It can be used for great good or wantonly wasted, depending upon the will of the person temporarily possessing it. Give yourself permission to exercise your own power for good right now.

"You must understand that there is no need for punishment… ever. God does not punish. That false concept was invented by your earthbound society. Tzaheer, the former priest, has progressed far beyond anger or bitterness toward your spirit. Allow yourself to absorb the first installment of the wisdom you've been out of touch with during your current Earth existence."

Spirit again switched gears, leaving me temporarily at a loss.

"Now that you can see forward and backward in time, Josh, I ask you to observe Roger's life in 1983."

I realized that Josh, though silent during Roger's encounter with the Egyptian priest, was still with us. Apparently he had absorbed it all with newly-augmented spiritual awareness.

"Look at the world through his eyes," Spirit continued, "and tell me who in his current life were also present in the life of that ambitious Egyptian. His number two wife returned to be with you, in a life of great hardship. Did any other people from that Egyptian experience appear in your Irish American life?"

"Yes."

"Who are they and what place, if any, do they hold in your New York life?"

"My neighbors: they were guards… fellow conspirators. I could not have pulled it off without their help."

"They were fond of you?"

"Yes, otherwise they would not have taken such risks."

"Observe the significance of this. You were not so bad as you believed yourself to be. There were people who loved and respected you enough to choose to be with you again, correct?"

"Right."

"Now to your current lifetime as Roger. Look carefully into the eyes of the people in this life. Do you recognize any of those people?"

"Jimmy."

"Who is Jimmy?"

Further questions revealed that Jimmy was the ship captain in his lifetime as an Irishman.

"What part did he play in the Egyptian dramas?"

"Well… he was a soldier then."

"Did he work for you?"

I should be used to this by now, but I still get a jolt every time Spirit pulls information like this out of his ephemeral hat.

"Yes."

"What was his name then?"

"Arak."

"Did you help him in any way?"

"Yes, I shared my food with him and gave him a tent and horses."

"Do you recognize Roger's mother in his current lifetime? Can you tell us why he chose that particular mother?"

"She was the priest."

"You both had to choose that relationship. The priest needed to work out his resentment. So you see, he wasn't as holy as you thought he was, after all, was he?"

"Right."

A Bitter Pill to Swallow

"Roger, how do you feel about your mother now?"

"She is still alive… living in Tennessee."

"Do you still feel bitterness towards her?"

"Yes."

"Will you now release that bitterness?"

Silent resistance.

"In doing that," Spirit asserted, gently but firmly, "you will free yourself, and also release the current incarnation of the priest from an ignoble urge to punish you. This positive energy may or may not affect your mother. That is her karma, not yours. Nonetheless it will be as great a blessing for her as was the forgiveness you just received from Tzaheer. It is only fitting that you, in turn, forgive him (her) for that human weakness. Can you really blame Tzaheer for seeking vengeance against the man who stole his servant and whose lies ruined his reputation?

"Umpf!"

That grunt sounded like the reaction to a body blow.

Spirit drove home the point, "Revenge is a waste. It never brings about justice. On the contrary, it prevents us from attaining rarer, more highly developed spiritual awareness. In seeking revenge, the priest proved his own lack of spirituality at that stage of soul growth."

"Spirit is quite the philosopher," I mused.

"Think of what revenge has done to the priest through his many lifetimes, Spirit continued. "Compare the power he enjoyed in Egypt to the petty ways in which your mother expresses her desperate need for it now. Revenge depletes power. In the meeting between lifetimes you and the priest dealt directly on a deep consciousness level. Reincarnating as your mother offered an opportunity to resolve the bitterness between you. That plan didn't work out too well, I gather. Neither of you could let go until now.

"Tzaheer's real moment of power came when he forgave you and freed you of guilt. When you finally release the bitterness and resentment against your mother, you will have completely wiped out that karma and can claim your own power."

Roger was no match for Spirit's unerring logic. "I get it! Okay, okay… tell me how. How do you go about forgiving someone who's made you miserable all your life?"

"It's not about forgiveness… the only thing you need to do is release the bad memories. Suppose you find yourself splattered with mud. How long do you want to sit around with mud all over you, wasting time and energy complaining about it? The most efficient way to get rid of it is to take a shower and wash it all down the drain. You were splattered with negativity. Imagine yourself being bathed with cleansing energy that washes away the negativity which has held you prisoner for so long."

"Easy as that, huh? I can do that, I guess!"

Silence… then a sigh of relief.

"Now, having released the negativity which has prevented you from growing spiritually," Spirit continued brightly, "aim all the love you are capable of sending to that Egyptian priest's present incarnation, whom you recognize as your mother. In order to accomplish this, you are not required to love her. Just beam cosmic love at her. Say anything that will permanently expunge any traces of guilt from your consciousness right now."

Seconds ticked away as Roger wrestled with a lifetime of embedded resentment and envisioned the concept of living without it.

"I'm free," he announced with the sigh of a man who had labored hard and finally completed a grueling task.

"Yes, you are free," Spirit confirmed, "totally free! You are free to exercise your full power, to have money, friends, a comfortable home, a good life. You are free to experience satisfaction from your work… to stand tall in others' eyes as an equal, freely employing your powers… all of them.

The Sheikh Unmasked

"Who was this guy… before?" I wondered.

As if in answer to my unspoken question, Spirit continued cheerfully, "In Egyptian life, were you a sheikh?"

"Yes"

"By what name were you known in that lifetime?"

"Sherrad."

"Do you understand that you could have gone to that priest and confessed your love for his serving girl. If you had offered him a fair exchange for her—horses, camels, jewels, silks, the outcome might have been different. Understanding your desire to make her your wife, he might just have struck a bargain and enriched himself at the same time. Your feelings of love for her were not wrong. Nothing is right or wrong except the judgments you make and how those judgments affect others. The choices you made were based upon the knowledge that, according to your customs, you were committing a wrong against the priest. With all your wealth and power you were still not sure of yourself, were you?"

"Right!"

"Release that guilt now, Sherrad. Let it all go.

"The Jai-ling priest is holding out his hand in friendship and love to you, Sherrad. Nine beings from the spiritual plane are here to escort the two of you, Josh and yourself, to the realm that you are now capable of enjoying.

"Before you go, I ask you to give Roger the advice that will serve him best, knowing full well the circumstances of his life. This will enable you both to achieve greater levels of consciousness, though of course you will not do it for that reason. Just tell Roger what he needs to hear right now."

"Be true to yourself," boomed Sherrad, "and deal fairly with everyone, whether you think they deserve it or not."

And now, Sherrad, as you embrace Roger in farewell, you have yet another choice. You now know how Roger has suffered in vain attempts to make up for your human sin. If you wish, you may choose to work with him as a spirit guide. Would that please you?"

"Greatly."

The arrangements were easily set up between the two of them and acknowledged with a curt "done!"

"Then, knowing your remorseless cycle of self-torment and revenge is at an end, go! Go, Sherrad… with your once and now forever friend, Tzaheer… to the greatest rewards you can experience at this stage of your development. Let there be no limitations based upon earthly thoughts and expectations."

I sensed rather than felt a slight energy drain in the room. The two former enemies were with us no more. Spirit wasted no time proceeding to the task at hand.

Roger was on his way to rest and recreation on a cosmic level.

"Open every level of awareness and receptivity to receive the gift you've earned," Spirit advised.

As Roger enjoyed the rejuvenation process, it seemed as if he grew in the process. He returned to so-called normal consciousness a changed man. His voice surprised me with its ease and confidence.

"Well, I guess it's a new era now," he smiled as he gave me a bear hug and walked away with a jaunty spring to his step. You'd never guess what bridges he'd crossed and what demons he'd sent packing in those two hours.

Bye Bye Bad Karma

Revelations in Review

Over the next few days incidents in Pat/Josh's life and the revelations revealed in the dialog between Roger and Spirit kept skittering through my thoughts. Something Tzaheer had said would pop to the surface at odd times. The deluge of esoteric knowledge revealed in these sessions with Spirit was turning into a massive pile-up of data. Sifting and sorting was once more in order.

Each voyage into another lifetime brings new revelations that must be integrated into my evolving concept of reality. Roger's session was laden with a wealth of knowledge. As an empath, I was deeply affected by his burden of guilt. Reflecting upon the details, I encountered many new truths that had to be dealt with. The more I learned the more I had to realign my understanding of life, spirituality… even the nature of karma.

Pat/Josh had lived in New York in 1912. This was the first time a client had landed in so recent a lifetime. As much as my friend, Hans Holzer had stressed their importance, researching details revealed during these sessions was not a priority. My primary concern was the spiritual truths revealed and the healing that occurred. However, Josh had mentioned so many dates and locations that it made sense to check them out.

Research revealed:

- *In 1912 plans for the Manhattan Bridge were completed.*
- *The "Dreadnaughts," the biggest ships in the US Navy, sailed to New York in 1912. Some dredging work had to be done under the Brooklyn Bridge to enlarge the channel in order to accommodate them.*
- *There really was a 125th Infantry that fought in France in World War I as part of the 37th Infantry.*
- *Mike's Garage did exist in Chelsea in the early '20s.*

As fascinating as it can be to find corroborative evidence of information revealed in these trips into other lifetimes, I still feel the spiritual breakthroughs trump facts and figures.

There were many new layers of reality to ponder. When Spirit introduced Tzaheer, I realized the bar had once more been raised. To more fully assimilate the revelations about the inter-connectedness of incarnations and spirit healings, even after returning to the spirit world, I wrote down what I could remember:

- *God doesn't punish anyone for anything. (Woo hoo!)*
- *Revenge cuts both ways. Inflicting pain upon another activates negative energy that creates even more bad karma.*
- *Even after returning to the spirit world, an individual incarnation can manifest, reach out, give and receive… teach and learn. This can happen even if another incarnation of that Spirit is alive and breathing here on Earth! (Wow!)*
- *Clients can meet with an enemy from another lifetime and, with Spirit's help, resolve whatever stands between them. Then, at long last, they can forgive each other and release the karma.*
- *There's a big difference between grudging attempts to love an enemy and beaming non-judgmental loving energy toward that person.*
- *Loving energy beamed out without attachment or expectations heals and nourishes both sender and receiver.*

How often people torment themselves because they had been neglectful, thoughtless, unappreciative, or unkind to associates or loved ones who are no longer around? They assume it's impossible to make up for mistakes of the past. Roger's Egyptian incarnation, Sherrad, was given the chance to make amends and receive forgiveness for sins committed thousands of years ago. It was beautiful to witness.

Bye Bye Bad Karma

Millions of people are unjustly held hostage by a vapor trail of centuries-old transgressions, clinging like spiritual barnacles acquired in other incarnations. It doesn't matter when or where real or imagined offenses occur. What matters is that untold good could be achieved without the restraints we place upon ourselves because of subconscious guilt. Think of the inventions, the projects, the miracles that could be created without those blockages. What a waste!

According to Spirit, most "sins" are negligible on the cosmic level. That must be why it is so easy to erase the karma that interferes with our freedom to develop.

How I've Grown

The role of observer in these alternate incarnations is far from passive. As silent witness I am alternately fascinated, confused, disturbed, stunned and/or enlightened. Before this Odyssey began I was arrogantly dismissive of the entire concept. That was before being gob-smacked by a full-blown spontaneous regression. Talk about a crash course to heal an attitude—ha!

During early sessions my clients and I learned together and grew in ways we could never have imagined. It is my ongoing privilege to eavesdrop on all these conversations between clients, their alternate incarnations and an infinitely wise Spirit presence. The times and places, as well as the personalities involved, are always surprising, contributing to often the most esoteric, otherworldly circumstances imaginable. I cannot help but learn from observation and hopefully absorb some of Spirit's wisdom while facilitating these events. How lucky can you get?

Chapter Twenty-Four
Heal at Your Own Risk

After consulting many doctors whose treatments failed to relieve her condition, Ellen decided to try a holistic approach. "At first the formulas and methods that were offered looked promising. There were raving reviews and testimonials of miracle cures. So I tried everything," she assured me, "and it just got worse. It seems like anything healthy is bad for me. Someone suggested my condition might be karma related, and gave me your card. Could I please make an appointment as soon as possible?"

I spent more time than usual in the orientation stage, describing the guided imagery and relaxation techniques we would be working with. I explained my mission... my agreement to work only with wise, loving Spirits who were committed to help us accomplish what we came here to do.

Our work with other incarnations confronts conflicts that impact upon the present lifetime and eliminates the accrued karma. The process is geared to the transmutation of events from negative to their highest potential for good according to Spirit's judgment. Next, we discussed the required agreement that there would be no pain. Finally we both were satisfied that she was ready to begin.

Contrary to my expectations, Ellen floated easily into a state of altered consciousness. We landed near an isolated cabin in a small clearing. She was drawn to a young blonde woman who was walking toward the cabin with a basket of herbs.

Vishya

I introduced Ellen and myself and asked her name.

"I'm called Vishya," she responded hesitantly.

With delicate questioning I learned she was barefoot and wearing a white frock with lots of petticoats.

"Can you tell me what year it is, Vishya?"

"1690."

"Are you married?"

"No, I live alone."

"Have you always lived here?"

"No, I came over."

"Came over from where?"

"Poland."

"What was it like living in Poland?"

"Hard."

"How old were you when you left Poland?"

"I was seven."

"Was there an adult in charge, someone to hold your hand," I asked, "to protect and guide you on the trip?"

"I didn't need my hand held."

Reluctantly, Vishya revealed that her parents sent her to the New World with a group of 50 children. There was no adult supervision. Her brief, matter of fact answers revealed that about 25% of the children were Polish, whom she knew only by nationality.

"Was your family religious?"

"Catholic."

"Was there a priest or a nun to help you on the ship?"

"There was an old woman."

"Did she speak Polish?"

"She spoke all languages."

"Did she teach you another language?"

"No."

Bye Bye Bad Karma

"Were you frightened?"

"Yes. But I was determined."

"Where did the ship land?"

"The coast of Boston."

"What happened when you got off the ship?"

"They put us in a community."

"What kind of community?"

"I lived in a house with the children."

"And what did you do?

"I sewed."

"You knew how to sew at seven?"

"Yes. You see, everyone had work to do. I was too little to do the heavy work, like carrying water and digging and hammering, but I thought maybe I could sew. I looked at the way things were made and I learned how… all by myself."

"Did you know how to cook too?"

"No, the pots were too heavy. I was only seven."

"What kind of things did you sew?"

"Frocks for ladies."

"What happened to the smocks after you made them?"

"The merchants in the town sold them."

"Did they pay you for the smocks?"

"They paid the orphanage."

Suspecting this might be a sore point, I changed the subject: "Did you miss your parents?"

"I wouldn't let myself feel it."

I wasn't sure how to help someone so young through such hardship. Finally, much to my relief, Spirit arrived.

"And now my dear Vishya," Spirit gently suggested, "let's go forward in your lifetime to the day you finally left the orphanage. How old are you now?"

"Fourteen," answered the youthful voice.

"Do you have a place to live now?"

"I found this abandoned cabin in a field out of the mainstream."

"What happened to the old woman on the ship?"

"She was burned." Young Vishya's voice registered fear as well as sadness.

"How did that happen?"

"I know how. She was burned because they were scared of her. They said she was a witch."

"Do you think she was a witch?"

"Yes."

"Why? Did she cast spells on people?"

"No, but she could cure."

"Vishya, that doesn't make her a witch," Spirit assured her. "Healing is a gift from God. God honors those who can cure people."

"I think I must be a witch too, because I was set apart."

"Who set you apart?"

"My mother and father."

"Did they think you were a witch?"

"They didn't care. They had to survive."

"Did they have enough to eat?"

"When the harvest was good."

"You're a wise young lady, so I'm going to ask you to do something most people your age couldn't possibly do," Spirit announced. "Imagine you're a grown woman with a beautiful, clever, much-loved little girl. There's no food and no way you can give her what she needs, what she deserves. Would you be selfish enough to keep her with you? That would condemn her to more and more misery… perhaps even death from starvation. What if you were told you could send her far away, to a place where she would be warm and fed, and perhaps have a chance for a better life? Think deeply, dear Vishya. What would you do? Could you love that child, the only beautiful thing in your life, enough to let her go?"

"Oh…" a half sob, half gasp shook Ellen's body.

"Open your heart Vishya and let yourself love your mother and father, who sacrificed everything for you. If you love them even one-tenth as much as they loved you, your heart will be overflowing."

Silent tears ran down Ellen's cheeks.

Mirror, Mirror

Without missing a beat Spirit switched gears. "It's told that witches have no reflection in a mirror. When you look upon a mirror what see you?"

"Myself."

"Does that not prove you are not a witch?"

"But methinks I must be…"

"Vishya, please tell me what makes you think you're a witch. What do you do that's witch-like?"

"I help people."

"How do you help them?"

"I just know what they need."

"There's a word for that—empathy. As an empath you can feel other people's feelings and their pain. That's how you know what they need. You are not a witch; you are psychic. It's a talent God has given you. Say it after me—I am psychic."

"I am psychic."

"And now I want to introduce you to your soul sister, Ellen. In her world common men and women have at hand more knowledge and understanding than hundreds of the most learned men in Boston could master in a lifetime. I'm asking her to open her heart and mind and share that knowledge with you, Vishya."

Ellen's voice, laden with gentle concern, came through. "It's the earthly things that are bothering you. You are not your hardships. You are far more than that. You have locked your pain inside, hidden it away to keep from hurting. But locked-up pain hurts the most. It prevents you from being who you truly are. When you let it go you will be free."

"Now, even though you insist I am not, I fear I must truly be a witch," Vishya cried. "A me that is not me speaks wisdom I have not. Surely that is witchery."

"It is your soul sister who speaks so lovingly to you, Vishya. She speaks heart-felt words to comfort you. Please listen very carefully and answer truly," Spirit continued. "If you were indeed a witch would you slave with needle and thread till your fingers bleed, your eyes burn, your shoulders ache and your head spins when you try to stand? Phah! A witch would chant a spell, snap her fingers and six dresses, nay, ten dresses sewn by unearthly hands would appear. Can you conjure that?"

Once again, I marveled at Spirit's mastery of the dialect.

"No. Never!" Vishya cried in dismay.

"Have you perchance cast evil spells on those who slandered you and turned them into trolls or hogs?"

"No." Ellen's body shuddered at the thought.

"Have you ever forced anyone to do your bidding against their will, or cursed, or put a hex on someone who caused you harm?"

"No!"

"Then repeat after me, 'I am not a witch.'"

"I am not a witch," she solemnly repeated.

"Now that you realize you are not a witch, let's go forward to a time when next you find yourself in need. One… two… three… Now tell me where you are and what year it is?"

"It's 1730 and I'm in my little cabin. I've made it into a beautiful, cozy home and I love it so. And I love the field. it's all abloom with flowers and herbs."

Rumors and Gossip

"Vishya, you have done so well. You have created a lovely home for yourself from cast-offs, thrown away scraps and pieces."

"That's why they call me a witch."

"Then you are aware of the whispers."

"How can whispers hurt me? It's only one or two… I think they're jealous."

"That's how it begins. It's time to move forward, to choose life instead of the fate that will befall you if you remain here."

"But I do heal people. They need me."

"What if you could live and work in a city, with more sophisticated people who would call you a genius instead of a witch?"

"How can I leave my sweet cabin and my field? I need to be right where I am."

"City people need your help too… and there are so many of them that you can do ten times—a hundred times—the good you can do here. There will be people who need you wherever you go."

"I need the land. I need the air. It's my connection to God."

"There is land at the edge of every city, and air as sweet as ever you breathe here. Soon it will be filled with the fragrance of your herbs and flowers. If you stay in this place all that you have created will be profaned, vandalized and destroyed. Your herbs and flowers will be trampled into the mud. You will not live to help people who desperately need you."

"I see now it would have been wise for me to move away, but it's too late. They've made their decision."

"We have come here to prevent dreadful things from happening to you!" Spirit declared.

"How? There's no way out. They tied a rope around my neck and dragged me to this pen. I'm bound hand and foot… can't move. They're going to do to me just what they did to the old lady."

"You have saved many children. There must be one father who is so grateful… who cares enough to return the favor. Let your spirit call out to one who feels obligated to you for saving his child."

"Most everyone I helped is poor. They can't help me."

"There must be someone who has a wagon… someone who has business in the city? He could transport you, your herbs, and the few things you cannot live without to a safer place. It seems a small price to pay for the life of a child."

"Oh, I think mayhap there be someone."

"You can gift them with all the possessions you cannot take with you as payment."

"Yes, they will be glad of it. There are provisions… things I've made, and clothing they can use."

"Listen now… hear that scratching? That is not an animal."

"Spirit magic again… and not a moment too soon," I exulted in my little sliver of consciousness.

"Good Mistress Vishya," came a raspy whisper, "can you inch a leetle closer to the stakes? Hold your wrists by this crack between the boards so I can cut the rope and free you."

"God's mercy, it's Samuel," she whispered.

Ellen's body writhed about as Vishya struggled to position her wrists by that tiny crack. Samuel's pocket blade easily slit her bonds and she was free. The moonless night cloaked the two of them on their quick dash to her cabin. They gathered all her necessities together and stashed them in Samuel's wagon.

Spirit once again took charge. "You will need money to start over. There is an elm tree at the edge of your field. If you dig on the northeast side three handbreadths from that tree you will discover a small wooden casque. It contains enough silver to see you through until you're settled, with three pieces of eight left over for the brave neighbor who risks his life to save yours."

"How…"

"Question not the love God holds for you."

A muffled sob was all she could manage.

Survival Training

"It will be necessary to create a protective identity for you so you can blend into your new surroundings," Spirit continued. "Mark how the brown spotted rabbit develops a pale coat to blend into a snow bank. Drawing upon your observations of nature, you will understand the necessity of the process. Without it there would be no rabbits, do you see?"

"Yes, I know of rabbits, and many small creatures who survive by hiding in plain sight."

"Now you have it… and so shall you master it! You will need a new identity and credentials. People who have never known someone like you will need reason to trust you. First, Samuel can ask a relative to vouch for you as one whose great skill has saved his child and many others.

"You will be asked how you learned so much about healing and herbs. In the Poland of Ellen's time are great universities. Scholars there study herbs and draw upon the wisdom gathered over the years by psychics and intuitives like you. Since you were born in Europe you can modestly say you studied there. It will be the truth, since as a child you did go to school and study. Remember all the things you learned in your short time in Poland.

"Next, you will need to find a proper place for your new home. When you arrive in the city let your inner knowing lead you. It will take you to a small cottage with an overgrown garden where you may be close to nature yet near enough to the city that people might readily reach you. You must put up notices in communal gathering places so people can learn where to find you. Memorize these words: 'European Herbalist.' Below that you will write: 'Ancient and modern secrets for health, long life and beauty.'"

"But how can I lie?"

"These words are carefully crafted so they do not lie. Did not those you healed live longer? Was not their health restored? Did not your balms prevent scarring? You know more about herbs than anyone in the whole Colony of Massachusetts, possibly in all of the colonies. Where and how you accumulated that knowledge is no one's business."

"But they will ask so many questions."

"When they ask you must look very mysterious and say, 'I studied for years with very wise instructors.' In Ellen's world that's called snob appeal."

That cracked me up. Spirit must be sifting through my brain to locate the proper words to make his point. "Down girl," I told myself. "you can giggle about that later!"

"But I didn't…" Vishya protested.

"Of course you did. Nature is the wisest of teachers. You have accumulated much of earth's great wisdom. Plants revealed many of their ancient secrets to you. There are no greater teachers on this plane. There is need to prove your worth and curry their goodwill. But no one need ever know that you are an empath and a psychic. They will attribute their miraculous cures to the advanced knowledge you gained from European masters. The deeper truth is that you brought much of that knowledge from another lifetime in Europe. You will not be lying. Rather you will simply tell the part of the truth they need to know in order to place their fate in your hands."

"What is truth and what is lie?" Vishya cried. "I'm frightened at the thought of leaving my whole life, everything familiar behind me. I know this life, these simple people… truth is truth."

"The witch hunters have already ended the life you know. There are truths beyond understanding and truths I can share with you. Open your mind and heart and listen well. There is no reason to suffer injustice and give up your life simply because society says it must be done. What you know of healing and what you have to give are far more important than local customs. Gifted people like you deserve to live.

"You see, we are all in control of our own destiny. When you came to this planet your spirit chose your parents. You chose the circumstances of your birth. During the birthing, and learning to live on this plane, your spirit began to lose touch with the wise soul that made that choice. When you found yourself in difficult places for reasons you could not recall or understand, you listened to others and began to absorb the traditions of the people around you. In order to survive you accepted their mistakes, beliefs and fears as truth. Soon you were cut off from the God that sleeps within you.

"The truth I offer you, Vishya, is this: Each and every one of us is a part of what you call God. Everything we do is either an affirmation or a denial of God—the maleness, the femaleness, the it-ness of God. It takes every sun and star, every planet, every rock, plant and living being upon every inhabited planet in the millions of universes to make up the body of God. You and I are much needed and valuable parts of God. Every hair on your head, every organ, every single corpuscle, is a part of God. Honor God by living your life well and enjoying it. Do good for people and help them in every way you can. Use your God-given talents, your fine mind and express your love safely, without fear.

When In Rome

"Heed the ancient wisdom of your planet: 'When in Rome do as the Romans do.' Even while appearing to do so you must yet remain intact within your own soul. Always be true to your own identity.

"You love plants and animals. Learn from them. Observe the way they employ protective coloration. There is an insect that looks exactly like a twig. Do you know why it does that?"

"To keep from being eaten?"

"Exactly! All I have urged you to do is to employ protective coloration. Clear?"

"Clear."

"If you don't survive you cannot do good works, can you? And if you do not survive the world will be much the poorer without the gifts you have to give. Vishya, will you accept our help?"

"I'm ready."

"As I count to three, you will find yourself in Samuel's wagon, on your way to safety and your new life. Together we will float through time and observe your life as if watching the gentry and countryside from the window of a coach. You'll glimpse yourself finding a simple cottage and transforming it into a haven for all in need. See yourself developing new survival skills, new friends and a thriving practice. See with your heart the grateful clients who brag that they were treated and cured by their famous European herbalist doctor. They almost don't dare to not get well."

A Fresh Start

Vishya acknowledged the unfolding plan as Spirit spelled it out with a chuckle and a sigh. Time spun ahead in seconds as she carved out a future she never could have imagined. It was truly Spirit in action.

After a moment of silence, Spirit acknowledged her achievement. "You have finally settled into a pattern of contentment and fulfillment. Feel how comfortable you are now that you have grown into your protective coloration. You may go to church or simply speak to God in your heart in ways only one who knows and loves you well can understand. You will live long enough to fulfill your need to help others. There is much beyond that simple basic plan that you will learn along the way."

Ellen let out a deep sigh of contentment. She was positively glowing.

"Let us go forward to see the fruit of your toil now that you're settled in your new home. What do you love most about your life,

Vishya?"

"Oh, my garden! I've expanded my knowledge of herbs, learned about plants native to this continent and this region to add to that which I already knew. There is so much to be done and so many who need me. They are very grateful for my help. My little shop is filled with love, with gifts I treasure, goodwill and loving kindness. I continue treating babies I once saved. They're now grown with children of their own. I am the most blessed of women!"

"With all those spiritual treasures clutched to your heart, let us go to the last day of your life in the body known as Vishya as I count—one… two… three."

"I'm ninety-five. I've just finished working on a patient. It's okay to go now because my assistant has learned all I have to teach."

"Good. You have trained her well and she knows it's your time."

"Yes, with her well-tuned gifts, she knew it beforehand, as did I."

"As soon as the patient with you leaves, take your assistant's hand and go quietly into your sacred garden. Speak to her the words that will comfort her when you go."

Closure

"It's your journey now, Elizabeth," Vishya assured her assistant. "You have the gift to heal. You have studied, practiced and learned to use it well. I'm proud of you. Use wisely all that I have taught you, but be ye open to learning yet more."

"Well spoken," Spirit encouraged. "And now simply float out of your body, Vishya. Cast aside your earthly limitations and let the knowledge of the universe flow into your expanding beingness. Allow the power you set aside temporarily in order to revisit the Earth plane to fill you as your awareness extends far beyond Earth imaginings. And now, please, would you look at Ellen's life and gift her with the knowledge she needs?"

"She's not in touch with herself. She keeps thinking she has to leave home."

"But she really doesn't, does she?"

"No, she's an enlightened spirit in a human body. I see white light shining through her… and she's floating."

"Oh, very high," Spirit affirmed.

"She will be released from her mental torment."

"Ellen's habitual thinking confuses the issues and obstructs the healing energy," Spirit explained. "The fear carried forth from that dreadful tragedy that happened in yet another existence has been entirely erased by your courage. Since you conquered that fear, Vishya, it will never affect Ellen again. When given the opportunity, you chose a beautiful, productive life that touched many lives in many positive ways.

"You have proven to Ellen that love awaits those with the courage to pursue it. She now understands that she need not live within the limitations that bound her to negativity and lack. Just as we helped you to make space in your life for the good and encouraged you to use your powers to create the world you deserved, so can you now help her to do the same. Please give her your best guidance and support."

"Love yourself," Vishya counseled sagely. "If you cannot love yourself, how can you love anyone else? Learn to love your pain as your teacher and simply push through the confusion. You need to allow yourself to connect with people and with healing foods and herbs. Surrender your pride. You need to feel deeply loved and give your love unstintingly."

"Thank you, Vishya. It is now your time to go onward to the wondrous realms awaiting you," Spirit announced. "Some very beautiful, noble spirit beings are waiting to escort you to the fullest level of existence you are capable of experiencing now. There, awaiting you, are opportunities to learn even more, to grow and continually expand. You will experience beauty and love to nourish your soul and be offered the freedom to flower and progress closer and closer to the oneness. You may remain connected with Ellen if you wish, work with her, help her, warn her of danger and be her guide. Would that please you?"

"Yes."

"Ellen, do you want to ask anything of Vishya before she goes?"

"Oh, I have fear for her going into the unknown. I don't know what that means, but I guess because she's a pioneer she'll survive."

"Fear not, my dear. She is beyond trouble now. She's moving ever closer to bliss… to supreme compassion, support, infinite love and understanding. She will be welcomed into a world of unfiltered communication and limitless opportunity."

"Will she come get me when it's my time?"

"I think that has already been answered. Now Vishya, it's time to agree upon a signal so that Ellen will know when you're near. Choose something that will catch her attention and help her stop listening to her fears, and listen to you instead."

"I want two signs… one for danger and one for opportunity," Ellen piped up.

"Sounds good," Spirit commented.

"Does it mean that when I start feeling this stuff in my stomach, Vishya is there with me?"

"Yes, she can be with you instantly… from any part of any universe," Spirit assured her.

"Do you feel that swelling of love?" Vishya asked. "And when you're walking down the street and the sun catches your eyes you'll know that I am there. I can also shine a little bit of light on things I want you to notice. Even when you're in your store it will be like something pops up and you suddenly see it."

"Oh, yes, I think I've already felt that sometimes," Ellen sighed.

"That's me!" Vishya chuckled.

Ellen was overflowing with contentment.

"And now we must let Vishya go to her reward," Spirit announced. "She's overdue."

"I'm going to be very sad to see her go, 'cause I grew to love her," Ellen sighed. "We've shared so very much, so very deeply. I opened my heart and soul to her. But, oh, I know it's time to let her go… and Vishya, don't stop till you get to the top."

"Okay, Ellen." Vishya's voice trailed off as she left our world behind.

Spirit quickly spun Ellen off to her perfect vacation spa and when she was fully restored, brought her (reluctantly) back to the body on my couch. "Float back to New York City, to the vehicle you know as Ellen."

"Oh please, Spirit, can't my friends stay there?" Ellen pleaded.

"They have their own work to do, but they can meet you there when you return to recharge from time to time."

"Oh, okay."

Once back in her current version of reality, Ellen brushed tears from her eyes and steadied herself.

"Now you know why you had such a bad reaction to herbs. It wasn't you; it was Vishya, who was tortured because of her knowledge of herbs. Now with her great joy, success, and sense of purpose embedded in your consciousness, that's all a thing of the past… no pun intended," I assured her.

"There's something I need to tell you," she murmured and then unburdened herself of a painful secret. Once persuaded it was not nearly as shameful as she had believed, she headed back out to embrace her New York existence—more confident, more peaceful, and more positive than she had been in years.

I had barely enough energy to swallow a glass of water and head for my power chair. "Thank you, Spirit, but please," I plead. "linger with me a moment more. That trip was almost as meaningful for me as it was for her."

An indescribable feeling of sheer aliveness engulfed me from crown chakra to toes, restoring me to my usual energetic self. I reached for a stream-washed citrine to ground me and calm the tingling of my hands. I rang my Tibetan bells and sent up prayers of gratitude. The unseen guides who shepherd me through these wild adventures had never felt so close or so real. Then with heart overflowing I repeated my prayer mantra, "I give thanks for the miracle that is happening right now."

Chapter Twenty-Five
The Importance of Being Open

Like many Americans, I once dismissed karma as either superstition or an archaic Indian version of purgatory. It seemed totally ridiculous to suffer over and over for sins of the past. Why waste time worrying about unknown events that are over and done with? It took the equivalent of a spiritual shock treatment to open my heart and mind about this particular subject.

Fortunately for me and for my clients, the spontaneous event that blasted me out of my complacency was followed by a Spirit-led crash course in karmic resolution. During my on-the-job training there was plenty of time to watch and learn. After I had enabled clients to relax and guided them into a state of altered consciousness, my only job was to remain open, connected, and to keep the energy flowing. Watching Spirit resolve the issues that caused "bad karma" was mind-boggling... but that was only the beginning!

The vast scope, ease and effectiveness of the work increased exponentially with each jaunt into other lifetimes. Unlike hypnotic past life regressions, these were not mere replays of past events with fixed endings. There was a powerful sense of immediacy and a knowing beyond temporal understanding that confirmed these were divinely inspired events.

The soul-expanding encounters with other incarnations Spirit so skillfully led us through grew ever more complex and meaningful over time. The relationships between clients and their alternate incarnations were deepening. Spirit taught them how to exchange information and brainstorm fresh, new courses of action with their new friends in those other life situations. The life-altering changes generated by their choices were so real they became deeply embedded in the consciousness of both incarnations. Positive changes in perception manifested in many ways from that point onward.

"Hold on, here!" my left hemisphere almost screamed at me between sessions, "How can this be?" It wasn't nearly as easy to remain open when I wasn't "on." The process of integrating these new revelations into what I thought I understood of reality was fraught with mental and emotional peril. Confrontations and experiences I could never have imagined sent me into a series of escalating spins, alternating between overwhelming confusion and pure joy.

Reality In Flux

Questions swirled away in my internal dialogue: "Who am I kidding? How can these things possibly be happening? Does this mean that even if something occurred in the past, it's not necessarily over and done with—frozen permanently in that pattern?" The fact that I had no Earth-based authority to turn to for confirmation complicated things. I was in uncharted territory. Perhaps this was how my pioneer ancestor, William Clark, felt forging ahead into the wilderness without landmarks or maps on his way to the Pacific Coast.

Each new encounter was replete with sensory overload and formerly inconceivable truths. We had to live through a whole phalanx of undesirable states of mind to reach the final resolution of our new reality. A great deal of faith and forbearance was required to survive in this whole new reality. Time after time I sent out a desperate SOS to the Universe. Thankfully, each plea for help brought a reassuring response and deft handling of the intimidating situation that ultimately made total sense.

I gave up all pretense of being in control. Spirit increased the pace and intensified the involvement with other incarnations when we were strong and well centered enough to comprehend and cope with it. Most of my questions were answered by the work itself.

In one of our Thursday night spiritual development classes a student asked, "If all this happened so long ago, how can anything change when we act out a different plot?"

"I'd like to know that too," I echoed, then, oops… I slipped unintentionally into altered consciousness. From that increasingly familiar, slightly fuzzy state I heard my mouth gently but firmly stating: *"Nothing that has ever happened to anyone, anywhere, any time is important!"* Stardust, my Number One Spirit Guide, drove her point home emphatically, as I drifted away.

Consciousness Redefined

> *"The only thing that matters is how the consciousness is affected… changed for the worse or for the better. By virtually living through a more positive version of what traditionally has been thought of as 'the past,' the consciousness is altered as surely as if the events had actually occurred. Now is now, whenever and wherever you are. Each and every new life event your other incarnations experience in their journeys with Spirit impacts upon the core consciousness. Those experiences and the changed perceptions become the new subjective reality and resonate across many incarnations."*

"But what about history, newspapers, tombstones?" came the very logical question from a class member.

> *"These re-scriptings do not change newspaper headlines or carved gravestones. We spirit guides consider them the futile attempts of Earth dwellers to capture and perpetuate their limited version of reality. Linear measurement of time*

is extremely primitive… crude record keeping. It's not much different from the knots cavemen tied in vines in their attempt to keep track of things. The only events really worth recording are the changes that occur in the consciousness.

"Visits with other incarnations produce an immediate, expansive impact on the core consciousness. That impact is reflected in the way you think and feel about your daily life and what you assume are past and future events."

I came back to the class to be greeted with excitement and wonder. A class member gifted with total recall filled me in on the essence of Stardust's mini lecture. For some odd reason this radically different concept seemed fittingly appropriate, logical and reasonable.

My students quickly assimilated this information into their rapidly changing understanding of "reality according to Stardust." These revelations were dropped so casually and whizzed by at such an accelerated pace there was no time to doubt or question them. Fortunately, they were captured on our tape recorder.

As best understood and accepted at this moment, my job is to stay open enough to allow these miracles to happen. Logic can wait. There will always be plenty of time to let these events marinate in my brain till they can be assimilated.

The extraordinary encounters, unorthodox techniques, the surprising teamwork and far-reaching resolutions achieved during these journeys into other lifetimes provide glimpses into the depth and complexity of the immortal human spirit. Each unique encounter reveals convincing evidence that it is possible to heal the unresolved conflicts (karma) we bring into this incarnation from other times, other places, other lives.

These sessions continue to venture ever further and penetrate more deeply into the human consciousness. They take us to spirit realms undreamt of but so welcoming and caring that no one who has ever been there will ever be quite the same.

Bye Bye Bad Karma

How many uncharted dimensions of consciousness remain for us to explore and to work with? There is so much to unlearn and relearn. If these remarkable ventures into other "nows" are any indication, the best is yet to come. Opportunities as limitless as infinity await those with the vision, heart and courage to remain open to the limitless possibilities of existence.

Are you ready?

www.ingramcontent.com/pod-product-compliance
Lightning Source LLC
Chambersburg PA
CBHW032040090426
42744CB00004B/75